P T

Passing the Flame

BY

DICK JONAS

EROSONIC

The songs we sang

About the planes we flew

And the people we knew

In the wars we fought

www.erosonic.com

EROSONIC
Chino Valley
Arizona

P T F

Passing the Flame

BY

DICK JONAS

ISBN 0-9657189-1-3

Published
by
Dick Jonas
EROSONIC
PO Box 1226
Chino Valley AZ 86323-1226
www.erosonic.com

Bodoni

You may have detected in the literary works I've produced —CD inserts, mainly, but also in *RBAAB: The Red-Blooded, All-American Boy* — that I have a mortal fear of white space. This book is no different.

I didn't want to overwork the pictures, so I went looking for some artwork with curlycues and flowing lines. It didn't need to have a message; it just needed to look pleasingly artistic. In my Mac G5's font library I found Bodoni ornaments.

✦ ❀ ❁ ❀ ⚘ ❁ ❀ ✾ ⚘ ❦ ❄ ❦ ⚘ ❁ ❀

At first, I scattered them everywhere in the dreaded white space. I made them big — up to 36 points. At that size, however, they overpowered the lyrics and background blurbs on the pages. So, I toned them down somewhat. I reasoned that 24 points was plenty big enough, and that 14 to 18 points would serve nicely in most cases.

Then my devious fighter pilot mind began to conceive some diabolical fun. Instead of scattering flowery, ornamental, random font letters all over the place, how 'bout I form them into cryptic messages. So I did.

Now, if you really do care what the messages say, you have three courses of action to choose from:

1. If your computer system has the Bodoni ornaments font, it's easy. Type them into a word processor document, then change the font to something readable, like Helvetica or Times.

2. You can do it the Sherlock Holmes way. Take a few educated guesses about what letter each symbol represents until you have enough of an alphabet to decipher everything. The Bodoni script above will get you started.

3. Or, you can send me an email or postal message and I will send you a table which shows each Bodoni symbol in a column, along with it's corresponding Helvetica symbol beside it.

There is a fourth option. You can simply appreciate and admire the tasteful — or, tasteless, if your head is someplace mine is not — artwork.

Parental discretion advised.

The prose and poetry in this book uses the warrior's vernacular and may not be suitable for children.

PROLOGUE, WITH ACKNOWLEDGEMENTS

The aim of this book, along with its predecessor and the associated CD albums, is to preserve and perpetuate the legacy of the warrior musician. They are the people who create and perform primarily what are known as fighter pilot songs. Not exclusively; one of my favorite songs in this collection is about today's biggest bomber, the BUFF. Irv LeVine has added two songs about tanks and the people who man the mighty Abrams.

No warrior ever undertakes a mission alone. If he succeeds, if he wins the battle, there are always others who deserve the medals along with him. Similarly, one never writes a book all by himself. Seventeen people helped me create this one.

The warrior musician legacy is made up of three elements: people, airplanes, and action.

The people are those who fly and fight, along with the support crews who keep them in the air, and those who write and perform the songs. I cannot think of a single instance where any of these warrior songs was written by someone who is not a combat veteran. There's just something about getting shot at that cranks off the creative juices. I think in particular of a touching ballad which came out of WWI about a combat flier and his airplane. The song is *Futures*, and it's in Chapter Nine.

My old friends of long standing in this genre of music made their inputs. I've already mentioned Irv LeVine, with whom I've shared five albums, up to now. He helped edit the book, as well.

Toby Hughes is about the best "lyricsmith" I've ever known. If you've got a tale that needs to be told, Toby has the words to do it. He appears solo on his own EROSONIC album, *Fast and Low*. His book, *What the Captain Means: A Song of the In-Country Air War*, contains the lyrics and stories for that album.

For years I've wanted to do an album with Chip Dockery. With #11 and #12, it came about. Chip is one of the nicest guys I've ever known. There is an arresting sincerity in his lyrics.

Not to be left out is James Patterson "Bull" Durham, God rest his soul. You can think of Bull as the vice-Patriarch of all warrior musicians. The head patriarch, of course, is Oscar Brand. Bull PCSed to Heaven in May of 2004, between our last recordings and the publication of this book. Special thanks are due the nice folks at Austin City Limits and to Kris Kristofferson for allowing us to use the intro Kris gave for Bull on the Vet's Day '92 Incountry show.

The Juvat Boys Choir is alive and active today in the 80th Fighter Squadron, Kunsan Air Base, Republic of Korea. Those who helped write this book are alumni of the Choir. I am proud that I, too, am a member, having earned my patch when I was assigned to the Headhunters in 1983-84. My fellow alumni who helped with the book and with the production of the *Headhunters* album include Jay "Jaybird" Riedel, Robbie "Shadow" Robbins, Tom "Nogas" Reichert, Scot "Gunny" Glass, Bruce "Big Fella" MacLennan, James "Taz" Merchant, Don "Loco" Malatesta, Jim "Tex" Ritter, Jon "Meat" Tinsley, Dick "Dixie" Corzine, Eric "Digger" Drake, and Dale "Skin" Flick.

Greg Anders brings a very special element of credibility to the stories herein with his comments about his father, Apollo 8 astronaut Bill Anders. The song *Bill Anders* appears in Chapter 11 *Come and Join the Air Force*.

And speaking of credibility, there's none more solid than that of Dos Gringos. Chris "Snooze" Kurek and Rob "Trip" Raymond, lived the life described in their songs. They both flew combat in the Viper in Southwest Asia.

Especially meaningful to me are the contributions by my daughter, Angela Jonas. She wrote the comments for her songs in Chapter Nine, *God Bless America*.

Kat "BD" Burkhead of *Fresh Out of the Box* has an interesting perspective on the mindset of a female combat pilot. Twenty-one combat missions in the B-52 qualify her to speak.

It's not only the authors, but the singers, too. One very special group of pioneering war ballad singers are somewhat different; they are girls. Known as *Fresh Out of the Box*, these veterans of modern air combat are Christina "Duke" Deibel, Kat "BD" Burkhead, Carrie "HARB" Reinhardt, Rebecca "Coyote" Muggli, and Bonnie "Sassy" Pucillo.

My old friend, Col (Ret) Ken "Bat" Krause wrote the A-10 blurb. More credibility; Ken did a Vietnam combat tour in the Phantom, and flew the Hog later in his career. We've been friends for 38 years.

Mary Jonas, my #1 Roadie, best friend and beloved wife was, is and will continue to be a part of this undertaking. A former English teacher, she helped greatly with the spelling, grammar, and syntax. She handles the tech aspects of our singing gigs, and sings with me, as well. I love that woman!

Geoff Mack is the lyric genius behind the "I've Been Everywhere" craze. Erosonic has several different fighter pilot versions of it on four different albums. There are three in this book, and another in its predecessor, *RBAAB: The Red-Blooded, All-*

American Boy. Geoff once gave me a cassette tape with all the commercial versions up to now. There are in excess of two dozen, and the subjects range from his own Australian travelogue to some reasonably racy physiological lists. Geoff and his lovely wife, Tabbi, reside in Sydney, Australia.

Had it not been for Bill Getz and his two excellent collections of *The Wild Blue Yonder: Songs of the Air Force,* there would have been far fewer songs recorded. I am grateful to him for his dedicated effort and superb workmanship.

I need to acknowledge an excellent piece of art. On page 12-28 is a stylized drawing of a Viper which conjures up a "Jaws of the sky" image. It was done by the young man who was crew chief of my Viper on my last tour of duty at the Kun. I've tried to locate him, but without success. Son, if you're out there, get in touch with me.

Emmit Brooks and I have a friendship which has grown out of our music business dealings since the late '60s. Except for #14, Toby Hughes' *Fast and Low,* all of the albums on the EROSONIC label were recorded at his studio, in Las Cruces, New Mexico. His brother, Jake Brooks, provided instrumental accompaniment to many of the 14 albums. Emmit's friend, Steve Smith, has also been a tremendous help with instrumentation. Emmit is the magician who makes me — us — sound so much better than we really are. I'll always be grateful for his expertise and his treasured friendship.

The pictures in this book came from a number of different sources. Miss Mary is an excellent photog and she took many of them. A lot of the photos are scans of patches and other insignia in my possession. Many have come from the internet. The F-86 on the cover of #12 *Passing the Flame* came from the website of Marcel van Leeuwen. The WWI Nieuport on the back cover came from Alex Mitchell at the warbirdsovernewzealand site. Keith Ferris graciously permitted the use of his painting of the Sabre vs MiG fight on page 13-14. As with the other book, many pictures came from the Air Force Museum website.

The airplanes are those seductive little machines known as fighters. In my generation that was the F-100 Super Sabre, the F-4 Phantom II, the F-105 Thunderchief, and the F-111 Aardvark. I was lucky enough to be on the cusp of the flame passing; I flew the F-16 Viper for my last five years of active duty. For the next generation, to the Viper we add the A-10 Warthog, the F-15 Eagle, the F-22 Raptor, and the F-35 which is yet nameless.

The generation which preceded mine flew the F-86 Sabre,

the F-84 (with several "Thunder" names, depending on the model,) the F-80 Shooting Star, the P-51 Mustang, the P-47 Thunderbolt, the P-38 Lightning, and the P-40 ("Hawk" names, depending on the model,). I've probably left some out; forgive me, and refer to *Give Me Operations* in *RBAAB*.

Action, the third element of the legacy, goes back to WWI, the conflict when airplanes were first used as combat weapons. The rest of the action has taken place in my lifetime — WWII, Korea, Vietnam, Central America, the Balkans, Southwest Asia, and the Cold War.

From those stages and the people who played upon them comes the legacy of the warrior musician.

Champagne Flight at the Kun, May '84

Someone else's Viper and crew chief.

CONTENTS
In CD album sequence order

Cold Warriors — *Album Seven*

7- 3	1. Cold Warriors
7- 5	2. O-1E
7- 7	3. F-4 Back Seater
7- 9	4. Rollin' In My F-105
7-11	5. Bobby Watson
7-13	6. My Husband's a Colonel
7-15	7. Cold Black D. C. Wall
7-17	8. Early Abort
7-19	9. Get Me Out of Vietnam
7-21	10. Robin Olds
7-23	11. The Chief
7-25	12. Warrior Bards
7-27	13. Kansas Flash
7-29	14. Yodel-de-O

Boozin' Buddies — *Album Eight*

8- 3	1. Boozin' Buddies
8- 5	2. Yay-Boo
8- 7	3. Airman's Toast
8- 9	4. Golden Jock Strap
8-11	5. Bennie Havens, Oh
8-13	6. Peacemaker
8-15	7. Roll Your Leg Over
8-17	8. Buff
8-19	9. Hey, Mr Taliban
8-21	10. The Last Fighter Pilot
8-23	11. Reunion
8-25	12. I Don't Want To Join the Army
8-27	13. Wake Island
8-29	14. What the Captain Means

God Bless America — *Album Nine*

9- 3	1. God Bless America
9- 5	2. America the Beautiful/This Land

9- 7   3. This Is My Country
9- 9   4. How Great Thou Art
9-11   5. Amazing Grace
9-13   6. Danny Boy
9-15   7. Marine Hymn
9-17   8. Ain't Gonna Rain No More
9-19   9. Futures
9-21 10. GIB Named Richard
9-23 11. Bless 'Em All
9-25 12. Teak Lead
9-27 13. TV Commercials
9-29 14. Drugstore Cowboy

Live At Leeuwarden — *Album Ten*
10- 3   1. Hey Mr Taliban
10- 5   2. Nickel On the Grass
10- 7   3. Son of Satan's Angels
10- 9   4. Korean Waterfall
10-11   5. Pull the Boom From the Gashole
10-13   6. Yodel-de-O
10-15   7. Thanh Hoa Bridge
10-17   8. Give Me Operations
10-19   9. Superman
10-21 10. My Father Was a Fireman
10-23 11. Wild West Show
10-25 12. Sally In the Alley
10-27 13. T. Mike
10-29 14. 322FS History Song
10-31 15. I've Been Everywhere
10-33 16. Ballad of Jeb Stuart
10-35 17. RBAAB
10-37 18. Crack Went the Rifle
10-39 19. Woody's Song
10-41 20. Swamp Fox
10-43 21. 322FS Fight Song
10-45 22. Aye-Yi-Yi-Yi
10-47 23. Banana Valley
10-49 24. Royal Goddam Dutch

Come and Join the Air Force — *Album Eleven*

11- 3   1. Missing Man
11- 5   2. Come and Join the Air Force
11- 7   3. Co-Pilot's Lament
11- 9   4. Buccaneers
11-11   5. ORI
11-13   6. Bill Anders
11-15   7. Sher-Babes
11-17   8. GIB
11-19   9. Delta Dawn
11-21 10. Bernie Fisher
11-23 11. One-Level Gunner
11-25 12. Rolling Thunder
11-27 13. Prowlin'
11-29 14. Holy Shit!
11-31 15. Singha Hero
11-33 16. Old O-2 Pilot's Tale
11-35 17. My Iraqi Hacienda
11-37 18. Don't Bust Your Ass Fighter Pilot
11-39 19. Tanker's Yodel

Passing the Flame — *Album Twelve*

12- 3   1. Passing the Flame
12- 5   2. I've Been Everywhere
12- 7   3. Lakes of Tally Ho
12- 9   4. Call Out the Goddam Reserves
12-11   5. ZPU Gunner
12-13   6. Doumer Bridge
12-15   7. Cav Tanker's Boogie
12-17   8. The Choir
12-19   9. Mamas Don't Let Your Babies
              Grow Up To Be Juvats
12-21 10. Goin' In For Guns
12-23 11. TDY Again
12-25 12. Sammy Small
12-27 13. I Wish I Had a Gun Just Like the A-10
12-29 14. Bingo Over Baghdad
12-31 15. A-10

12-33 16. Nipple On the Grass

Headhunters — *Album Thirteen*
13- 3 1. Twin-Tailed Lightning
13- 5 2. My Grandpa's a Fighter Pilot
13- 7 3. Yankee Air Pirate In Me
13- 9 4. Death Rains Down
13-11 5. Hit the Jets a-Runnin'
13-13 6. Strafin' 'Round the Mountain
13-15 7. Korean Waterfall
13-17 8. Air Force 801
13-19 9. Yankee Air Pirate
13-21 10. Son of Woody Juvat
13-23 11. Drag Index On the Rise
13-25 12. Freedom Bird
13-27 13. We've Been Everywhere
13-29 14. Juvat History Song

7

Irv LeVine

Cold Warriors

Dick Jonas

With deadly precision these two fighter pilots sing about how it was. This is a must-have CD. . .

Mark Berent

This is the real thing. It'll tell you more than a thousand books about war. Vet or not, you need to have this CD in reach. . .

Oscar Brand

EROSONIC   Album Seven

Major Irv Le Vine flew the F-105 Thunderchief in the Vietnam war. He was assigned to the 388th Tactical Fighter Wing at Korat Royal Thai Air Force Base, Thailand. Ninety-nine of his missions were over North Vietnam, and 44 of those were in Route Pack VI in the Hanoi area. One of the elite 40% minority of Thud pilots who actually completed 100 missions, he flew his hundredth on his birthday in 1968. He returned to the States and flew the F-111 Aardvark until retiring from the Air Force in 1972. After that, he attended Texas A& M and became a veterinarian; he runs his own clinic in Mountain Home, Idaho. Irv is a licensed parachute rigger and a skydiver with 212 jumps; he is a graduate of the Army's Airborne Jump School at Ft Benning, Georgia. He is a scuba diver, a dog trainer, and a singer and writer of songs. Irv's decorations include the Silver Star, 3 Distinguished Flying Crosses and 16 Air Medals.

Dick Jonas flew 125 air combat missions in the Vietnam War. An F-4 Phantom II jet fighter pilot, he was assigned to the 8th Tactical Fighter Wing Wolfpack at Ubon Royal Thai Air Force Base, Thailand, from September of 1967 to May of 1968. For his acts in the Vietnam War, he was awarded the Air Medal 13 times and the Distinguished Flying Cross three times. After 22 years service, he retired from the United States Air Force in 1986 as a Command Pilot, holding the rank of Lieutenant Colonel. He is a teacher, a writer, a guitar-player, and a singer. He also flies.

7 0 1   Cold Warriors

> Cold warriors, cold warriors
>
> If it's cold, then it ain't war say the living and the dead

We kicked Hitler's ass and we left him laying dead

Four months later dropped the atom bomb on Tojo's head

From the Baltic to the Black Sea the iron curtain fell

And the peace we thought we'd died for became a living hell

> Cold warriors, cold warriors
>
> The peace we'd fought and died for became a living hell

North Korea would not admit the bloody war was cold

They destroyed the peace that was barely five years old

The plowshares we had meant to build became a bloody sword

The price was 33,000 lives but the peace was restored

> Cold warriors, cold warriors
>
> For 33,000 precious lives the peace was restored

Ten years later Vietnam became a bloody scene

The Army and the Air Force, the Navy and Marines

Fought the battle, gave their all, a half-a-million strong

And watched their buddies blown to bits in a hot war 10 years long

> Cold warriors, cold warriors
>
> We watched our buddies blown to bits in a
>
> hot war 10 years long

Kuwait fell one summer's day to Saddam Shit Hussein

The U. S. went to war on the Asian desert plain

Colin Powell, Stormin' Norman, Chuck Horner, too

Drove Saddam back to Baghdad with a hell-rain from the blue

> Cold warriors, cold warriors
>
> Drove Saddam back to Bagdad with a hell-rain from the blue

"Cold war" is a gruesome lie, ask the fighting lad

From Heartbreak Ridge to Khe Sanh and downtown Baghdad

When the bullets and the bombs are real, the blood flows rich and red

'Cause if it's war, then it ain't cold say the living and the dead

Cold warriors, cold warriors

If it's war, then it ain't cold say the living and the dead

. . . it ain't cold . . .   *Dick Jonas*

Those who gave their lives, health, well-being, and loved ones would not call it *cold* war, I think.

This song came more slowly out of the hopper than others I have written. I set out to write it as the title song for mine and Irv's new album. I got through the chorus initially, cooked up a tune . . . then, ran into a brick wall. I thought it was a poor idea, I didn't like the tune, and the guts just wouldn't come. So, I laid it aside for about three months. Then one day, I picked it up again and the damn thing practically wrote itself. I think it's one of my better efforts over the years.

B-58 Hustler

Though she never fired a shot in anger, she helped keep the enemy
at bay for 50 years. Look at those lines; pretty thing, ain't she.

702 The O-1E

CHORUS

Oh, the O-1Es go flying along the mountain track

Across the jungle and along the shore, and some just don't
come back

From high above I see him, he's down there by those trees

I'm up here in my Thunderchief, and I don't think he sees me

Good morning up there, fast-mover, this is Twinkie oh-one-three

I'm your FAC today, it's a fact I say; I'm in this O-1E

I'm gonna mark your targets and call your BDA

Now, don't you miss, or I'll be pissed; that's all I've got to say

Hey, both of us are pilots, we're all that we can be

He's not to blame, but I wouldn't trade planes; 'cause he's
flying an O-1E

CHORUS

He's got the job of 'bird dog;' he's not a fighter jock like me

He's the guy in the sky most likely to die 'cause he's flying an O-1E

I ride a Martin Baker; he sits on his flak vest

We both do a job for Uncle Sam, but I wonder who's the best?

I drop six 750s, they really leave big scars

He fucks around down close to the ground with
grenades in Mason jars

A thousand rounds of ammo, my gatling gun is mean

He thinks it's swell with a hand full of shells and an old AR-15

Now, the O-1E's an aircraft that most of us forgot

But it's really the 'most' and I'll raise a toast when I'm back at old Korat

Oh, the O-1Es go flying along the mountain track

Across the jungle and along the shore, and some just
don't come back

7-5

Too many didn't come back

Oh, here's to the O-1E

Yes, here's to the O-1E

. . . down close to the ground . . . *Irv LeVine*
    When a pilot owes a debt, he pays it. *The O-1E* was written for one of the many brave rascals who flew that tiny defenseless bird — in this case Jonathan Myer. Jonathan, by the way, is a writer and singer of songs in his own right. I once referred to him as a "grunt." I mean, after all, he didn't fly fighters over there, so, therefore, he was "something less." In my moment of conceit I had besmirched his character, at least in my mind. The brave men who were Forward Air Controllers were our eyes and ears, and because of their unselfish efforts we were able to put our bombs in places where they'd do the most good. O-1E pilots didn't have the luxury of speed, armor nor firepower to help them survive. All too many of them didn't. So! This song is a tribute to ALL those brave men, living and dead, who hung it out at the controls of the little O-1E — and especially for my friend Jonathan Myer.

O-1 Bird Dog
Patriarch of the FAC birds

7 0 3   F-4 Back Seater

I'm an F-4 back seater, I ride in the rear
Won't nobody tell me how I got back here
They say I'm a pilot and that's really cool
But I think down deep I broke somebody's rule

He does the takeoffs, his landings all crunch
I hang on tight so I don't lose my lunch
I tickle the beads until we get back down
And he gets real pissed off when I kiss the ground

       I'm an F-4 back seater and a long way from home

I got me some RHAW gear and a small TV, too
But the channels I get ain't so pleasant to view
I gotta find someway to get out of this pit
I feel like a mushroom in the dark — and deep shit!

They gave me a handle and I hang on tight
When he says, "break left," he ALWAYS goes right
I like that handle, it's something I use
Without it, I'd be just one big goddam bruise

       I'm an F-4 back seater and a long way from home

Some call me a GIB and some call me a Bear
 I don't mind the names — it's just riding back there
I try to control it the best that I can
But I can't get used to being called a pit man

I love Martin-Baker's shit-hot rocket seats
I get to go first and I think it's so neat
He's in a bad way, but I am much worse
'Cause the Jolly's got orders to pick him up first

      I'm an F-4 back seater and a long way from home

The boom is above me, the gashole's behind
I can see real good at three and at nine
But one thing I hate about this goddam pit
Looking straight forward I cannot see shit!

Yeah, I'm a back seater, I sit in the rear
Don't much touch the throttles and never the gear
I'm mostly real quiet but I want to shout
Let me fly up front so's I can see out

      I'm an F-4 back seater and a long way from home

We carry rockets and bullets and stuff
2000 pounders — we think we're so tuff
CBUs, snake-eyes, and missiles and nape
And this bastard goes like a scalded-ass ape

Night flying scares me, the MiGs and the flak
I just hate riding my ass in the back
When this tour is over and I go back home
I'll get me a Thud so I ride all alone

      I'm an F-4 back seater and a long way from home

F-4 Phantom II

Another Vietnam workhorse

Rhino   *Dick Jonas*

Another generation called her 'Big Ugly.' I guess maybe she wouldn't win any beauty contests, but she was such a lovable old girl. When the chips were down, she could kick ass and take names with the big boys.

Not only did she fight the grubby little hot wars, she helped the BUFFs keep the Cold War's peace as well. She was on the front lines in the Desert wars, too. I liked flying her because she did it all — ground attack, air combat, intercept, and nuke penetration at low altitude and high speed.

I never wanted to see the back seat again. But I did; I wound up on IP duty at Luke before I left her for good. I learned to fly her five times. RTU (Replacement Training Unit — the schoolhouse) for the pit, RTU for the front seat, the Fighter Weapons School, CIS (Central Instructor School) at Luke, and finally, recurrency training after my staff tour. I learned more about her as an instructor than I ever did as a student.

. . . a long way from home . . .   *Irv LeVine*

This one was a labor of love. A love for the song. A love for
the fun of writing the words and knowing they fit; and a love
that one fighter pilot has, out of respect, for a brother warrior.
Using the tune from the old WWII song, *I'm A Lousy Co-Pilot*, I
zeroed in on the back seat of the mighty F-4 Phantom. Here's a
young, eager, 'go-to-hell' pilot (Dick Jonas) who finds himself
peering into a radar scope instead of the bomb/gunsight he'd
wanted and expected. While he's doing his best to keep the guy
in the front seat alive and serving his country, he can't help but
have the typical thoughts you'll find in this song. I had a lot of
choices for names and could have called it *The Bear's Lament,* or
Why a GIB Growls, or even, *The FIR Flies.* But, *F-4 Back Seater*
fit the best. The listener/reader can readily picture the pit man's
frustration from the start and the verses will make him smile —
just as they did Dick. :)

Fox-Fo-Echo on Bear escort duty

The Soviets used to send long range bombers to skim the edges of
our air defense boundaries in the North Atlantic. It was part of the
cold war play book. The Phantoms played it very well; nobody in this
game ever got shot. The big fellows did not fare so well, however.

704   Rollin' In My F-105

I'm just an ordinary guy. That's all I'll ever be.
But I didn't feel quite so ordinary when my grandson said to me
"Grandpa! Were you ever in a war? Or were you scared to fight?
Tommy's grandpa said he didn't but he marched for
     peace and right."
Well, I didn't know what to say at first, then it all flooded back to me.
Those flights at dawn, those men now gone, and no real victory.

    I was rollin' in my F-105, back rollin' in my F-105
    Out across the Bac-9, I was sure feelin' fine
    I was rollin' in my F-105

I told him 'bout those early morning briefings
How Roscoe would snooze and would snore
How the briefers made us sweat, oh, I can hear those bastards yet
As they briefed on Hanoi once more

I told him 'bout those early rollin' takeoffs
The bullets, the bombs and the gas
How we'd take off in the night, when we'd get a burner light
And how it would kick us in the ass

    I was rollin' in my F-105, back rollin' in my F-105
    Out past Mobile Control it was good for my soul
    I was rollin' in my F-105

I told him 'bout those join-ups in the weather
        the tankers and old Thud Ridge
How it never brought us joy when the target was Hanoi
Southeast of the Hy Gia bridge

The MiGs, the SAMS and the ack-ack, "I'm hit! I'm hit! I'm goin' down."
How we'd heed that pilots call but we couldn't help at all
And another Thud soon hit the ground

        Then I went rollin' in my F-105, back rollin' in my F-105
        Oh, we only made one pass and if we didn't bust our ass
        We'd go rollin' in our F-105

I wanted to tell him a lot more, but then I saw it would keep
Some good friends bought the farm but I hadn't come to harm
And my grandson had fallen fast asleep

        Then I was rollin' in my F-105, back rollin' in my F-105
        Out across the Bac-9, I was sure feelin' fine
        I was rollin' in my F-105

        Yeah! I was rollin' in my F-105, back rollin' in my F-105
        Though it's been quite a while it really made me smile
        'Cause I was rollin' in my F-105

Photo courtesy of Marty Case

F-105 Thunderchief

Last Thud out of Itazuk'. Somebody turn out the lights . . .

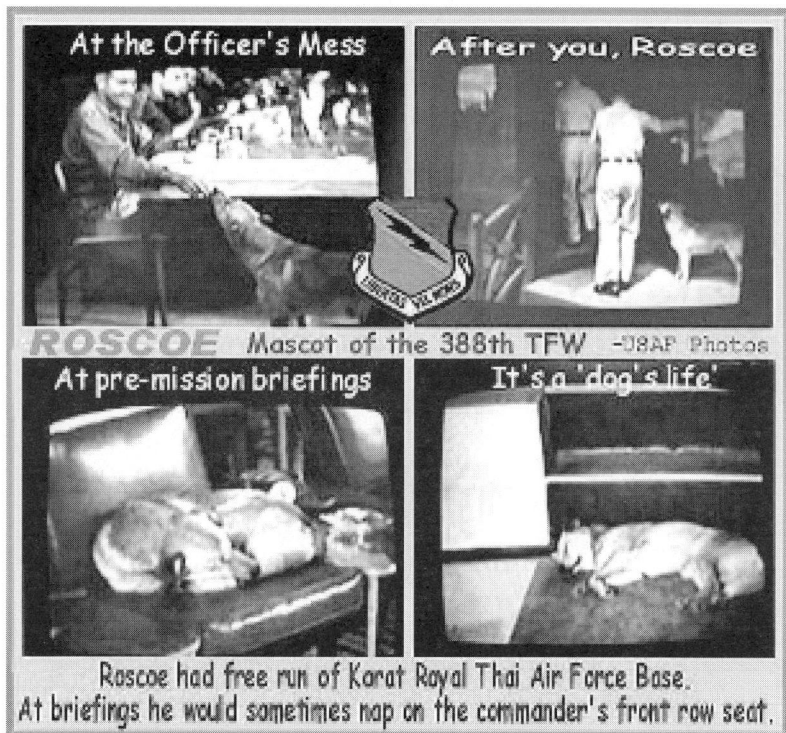

At the Officer's Mess

After you, Roscoe

ROSCOE   Mascot of the 388th TFW   —USAF Photos

At pre-mission briefings

It's a 'dog's life'

Roscoe had free run of Korat Royal Thai Air Force Base.
At briefings he would sometimes nap on the commander's front row seat.

... *ordinary* guy ...   *Dick Jonas*

I don't think I've ever met an *ordinary* Thud jock. Robbie Risner, Billy Sparks, John Piowaty, my pickin' and grinnin' bud, Irv LeVine — *none* are ordinary. I'll never forget ingressing to downtown Hanoi behind a gaggle of 16 Thuds. I saw one of them take a SAM in the underside of his left wing root. Even the mighty Thunderchief could not hold together under a direct hit like that. It started burning and coming apart. I didn't see the pilot eject, but on the way back out I heard the conversation over guard channel as his wingmen talked to him on the survival radio. His last words were, "They're all around me." That was late 1967, maybe early '68. He spent the next five years as a prisoner.

Their tour length was the same as mine: a year, or 100 missions over North Vietnam, whichever came first. I don't have to tell you that it takes monumental courage to keep going back in the face of such danger.

Uncommonly *extra*ordinary is what I would call them.

... **Roscoe** ...   *Irv LeVine*

None of his pictures do him justice. Most are faded and indistinct. But his memory is crystal clear in the minds of anyone who came in contact with him. Woe to the FNG who tried to keep him out of the O'Club, from cadging a ride in a vehicle, or sleeping in the commander's chair in the briefing room. Roscoe was unassuming, but seemed to know he was favored by all the pilots in the 388th Wing.

In 1971, some dipshit base commander tried to have him euthanized along with all the other dogs on base, but Roscoe survived. It was apparent that the troops were more in favor of having the base commander euthanized.

So, Roscoe stayed. He survived two deadly heart worm attacks,and, of course, he was over fed as everyone wanted to give him a tidbit. Hundreds of tidbits a day adds up to a lot of calories and Roscoe was no different than his human counterparts in that department.

Where he was different was in his ability to discern tough missions from milk runs, at least in the minds of every combat pilot there. If he slept through a briefing, it'd be a milk run. If he stayed awake, ears perked, it was going to be a bitch. Somehow, he knew. Superstition? Nonsense? Clairvoyance? I don't suppose we'll never know; but Roscoe and his karma will live as long as there's a 388th fighter pilot around to remember him.

He died of old age in 1975 and is buried at Korat Royal Thai AFB in a marked grave. Hand Salute! — for an old and trusted friend ...

705 Bobby Watson

I work for Bobby Watson, Bobby Watson works for me
He came across the ocean just to fly the F-4C

    Launched himself one Tuesday morning
    David Brooks upon his wing
    Airborne eleven minutes, Colonel Bobby did his thing

Tup Two, your Phantom's burning; tell me, whaddya think of that?
You got flames around your tailpipe, I bet you're nervous as a cat

    Hey, Wayne Stout, read me the checklist
    Tell me what am I to do
    If I dump it in the ocean, you'll be swimming with me, too

I love the fucking Air Force, the Air Force loves fucking me
There goes my tanks and rockets to the bottom of the sea

    How can I face Colonel Whiskey? Take me back to CCK
    I love the fucking Air Force, the Air Force loves fucking me

    . . . There's a fireball down there on the runway . . .

. . . fireball down there . . .   *Dick Jonas*

Bob Watson was my Ops Officer in the 44TFS Vampires at Kadena in the early 70s. We were TDY at Ching Chuan Kang Air Base, Republic of Taiwan.

Bob was #2 in a two-ship one crisp morning, giving Dave Brooks a flight lead check. Shortly after breaking ground on takeoff, Dave advised Bob that there were flames licking out the aux air doors on the belly of his bird. Bob turned immediately for the water to punch off the external stores. Then, as control deteriorated rapidly with the loss of the utility hydraulic system, he manhandled the plane back around for an opposite direction approach to the south runway. On short final, with no control now, the airplane began a roll very close to the ground. The crew hit the silk. Bob's 'chute popped and his feet hit the ground, just that quick.

The aircraft wound up looking a lot like the one in this photo. Except, the engines, at full power, tore loose and squirted themselves out the intakes, impacting near the infield mid-point. There was a small guard shack adjacent to the runway. I can imagine the instantaneous fright of the young ROCAF guard inside as the airplane hit the ground, exploding and sending those two big GE spools at full roar right past his ears. I expect he needed to go home and change his pants.

F-4 Phantom II

Just a wee bit the worse for wear. Thereby hangs a tale, I'm sure.

706 My Husband's a Colonel

CHORUS
Sing a little bit, drink a little bit follow the band
Follow the band, follow the band
Sing a little bit, drink a little bit follow the band
Join in our happy song

My husband's a colonel, a colonel, a colonel, a very fine colonel is he
All day he makes plans, he makes plans, he makes plans
At night he comes home and makes me
CHORUS

My husband's a major, a major, a major, a very fine major is he
All day he chews ass, chews ass, chews ass
At night he comes home and chews me
CHORUS

My husband's a captain, a captain, a captain, a very fine captain is he
All day he fucks up, fucks up, fucks up
At night he comes home and fucks me
CHORUS

My husband's a lieutenant, a lieutenant, a lieutenan, a very
        fine lieutenant is he
All day he eats shit, he eats shit, he eats shit
At night he comes home and eats me
CHORUS

RHIP *Dick Jonas*

If memory serves, I first heard this song while stationed at Langley AFB VA, in the mid-seventies. I was there doing my rated sup tour as a personnel puke. I was a major clerk in the candy store, helping to assign pilots to cockpits. EVERYbody was my friend — until I sent a hot rock, supersonic jock off to fly the Oscar Deuce or to live with the Army as a ground FAC (Forward Air Controller) or an ALO (Air Liaison Officer - like a FAC, only with more rank.) Then, I was the quintessential asshole.

It was a good tour of duty, though. In the personnel (I had trouble remembering how many "l's" and how many "n's" in "personnel") business, I learned that the Air Force was much bigger than the cockpit. It was long days and hard work, and a royal pain in the ass to try to please everybody up and down the chain of command. But, I rubbed elbows for three years with some of the finer officers and NCOs in the blue suit business.

To the best of my recollection it was Tom Coney, an F-4 combat WSO, who taught it to me. It never dawned on me to ask him where he got it. Coney knew a lot of stuff like that, and not just songs. He was one of the brigthter WSO's I ever came across.

It's a rousing sing-along song, and when it's done at a rowdy party I usually get a lot of help.

Air Force Officer Rank — Low To High

It's a long way in between.

7 0 7   Cold Black D. C. Wall

By that Cold Black D.C. Wall I heard a young girl calling
She said, "Daddy are you here or far away?
When you left both me and mom, for that far off Vietnam
You promised that you would come back some day."

"And, oh, how I wish you would come home
So things would be like before you'd gone
We would laugh and play and sing
And you'd push me on my swing
It's so lonely here at home for me and mom."

From that Cold Black D.C. Wall I thought I heard him calling
Saying, "Darling, dry your eyes for I'm right here."
Though I tried to make it back, Fate shot me off the track
And this is as close as I could make it, dear."

"And, oh, how I wish I could come home
So things would be like before I'd gone
We would laugh and play and sing
And I'd push you on your swing
And I'd never, ever leave you and mom."

As I stood close by that Wall an inner voice kept calling
And my heart went out to all who'd lost someone
Though the many years have passed their love and hope still lasts
It's so lonely for the one's who've lost someone

And, oh, how I wish they'd all come home

So things would be like they were before

We would laugh and play and sing, and our hearts would all take wing

And we'd all forget that awful Vietnam War

    We'd all forget that awful Vietnam War

The Wall   *Irv LeVine*

    The "WALL" says it all. It talks to you. It may be cold and black and seem to be just sitting there but it whispers to anyone that cares to listen. It did to me. I was told I'd cry when I saw the wall and thought of my lost comrades . . . those I knew and those I'd never met. I didn't cry. Men don't cry! Well, don't you believe it. If they don't shed tears down their cheeks, many cry 'inside.' The tears are as real as those that stream down a mother or father's face. There is no shame to shed tears for our lost loved ones, of course, but I was fascinated by the whispers that seemed to come from The Wall. They told a story that I needed to put on paper and to sing. I did both.

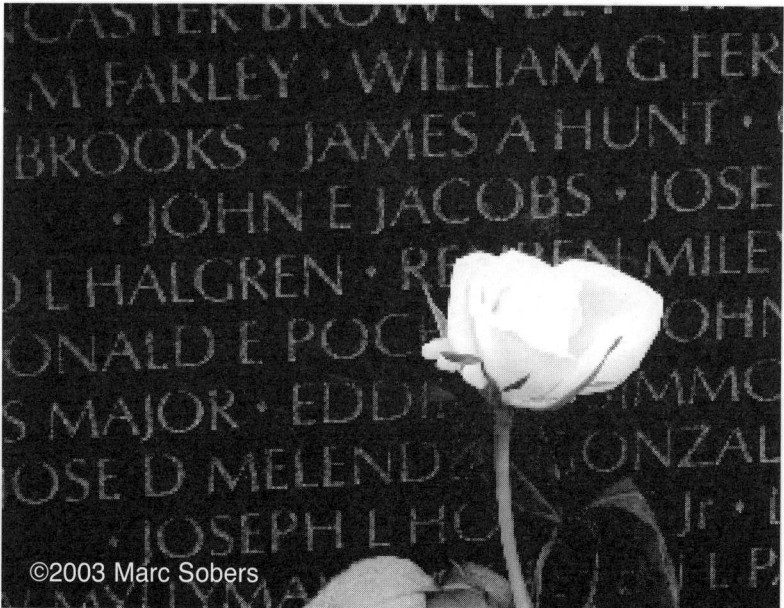

©2003 Marc Sobers

Never forget. Not ever.

Special thanks to Marc Sobers for an outstanding photo of the Wall.

708 Early Abort

Author unknown. Air Force traditional. Via Bill Getz in *"The Wild Blue Yonder."* Arrangement ©2002 Dick Jonas. All rights reserved.

My name is Colonel Whiskey, I'm the leader of the Group
Step into my briefing room, I'll give you all the poop
I'll tell you where the commies fly and where they like to roam
I'll be the last one off the ground, the first to come back home

> CHORUS
> Early abort, avoid the rush; early abort, avoid the rush
> Early abort, avoid the rush
> Oh, my name is Colonel Whiskey, I'm the leader of the Group

I'm sure you've heard of nightmares and all that they can do
Follow me down to the flight line, you'll see they're far from true
The pilots they are ready, but let the leader shout
And all those bastards yell at once, "My gyros won't check out!"
> CHORUS

We fly those bloody 102's a million miles an hour
We fly 'em in the rain and fog and in the bloody shower
And we fly so fast it fills us with alarm
Lose a bloody rivet and you've surely bought the farm
> CHORUS

We fly those bloody 102's at ninety thousand feet
We fly them through the rain and fog and through the bloody sleet
When we're flying bloody high, we're feeling awfully low
Lose the cabin pressure, it'll be an awful blow
> CHORUS

Now I'm sure you know about those people up at wing
Every night in the O Club you'll hear how well they sing
In words they fight a helluva war, they want some combat, too
But give them half a chance to fly and here's what they will do
CHORUS

The war is finally over and we're back in the U. S. A.
We fly and play the war games and do what the generals say
But when we have another war and they send us overseas
To hell with all them generals and those other SOB's
CHORUS

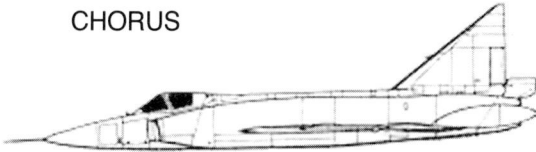

Colonel Whiskey   *Dick Jonas*

In a lot of the songs we sang, the odd, random colonel
would pop up. I sought to bring some consistency to the event by
choosing a name with color and flamboyancy. None suited so well
as my commander at Kadena Air Base, Okinawa, Colonel Bill
"Whiskey" Weiger. I don't know that he ever flew the F-102, but
he certainly knew what to do with a Phantom! Bill was a rarity
in my Air Force. He spent upwards of 25 years simply flying the
line. Most officers who make it to lieutenant colonel have gone off
to a "career broadening" staff job somewhere along the way. Not
him; he just flew his pants off in such machines as the F-86, the
F-100, the A-1E, and the F-4.

I guess he led a pretty exciting, if not profoundly charmed,
life; he was referred to as an F-100 ace, having crashed five of
them along the way. Toward the end of his tenure as commander
of the 44th Fighter Squadron, the Vampires, he was promoted to
bird colonel. He achieved it without having a college degree. Not
too many guys ever did that. But, after the promotion, he filled
the square.

He was an excellent leader in those days. He hasn't lost
any of it. I was privileged to have my ass chewed by him at the
most recent reunion of the Itazuke Afterburners. Not the first by
a damn sight, and if we both live long enough, likely not the last.

709   Get Me Out Of Vietnam

I was just 18 when they drafted me and sent me off to basic
They yelled a lot and wound my clock to see if I could take it
They sent me off to Vietnam, they said you'll make good money
We'll send you on to old Saigon, the weather there is balmy
>   CHORUS
>   Get me out of Vietnam; hey, I'm too young to bury
>   Take me back to the USA, make it cash and carry

I met some girls and they liked me 'til I ran out of money
I caught a ride in an old Humvee, went off to see the country
They dropped me off at old Pleiku; they said this is the front
I thought they'd call me soldier, but they only called me grunt
>   CHORUS

I met a lovely, lovely girl, half French, half Vietnam
And there I was away from home across that great big pond
That very night old Charlie came a-poppin' with his mortar
He seldom missed, he seemed real pissed; didn't know
>   she was his daughter
>   CHORUS

Don't mix girls and mortars if you don't want to die
Go on home across the foam to mom and apple pie
Get me out of Vietnam; I promise evermore
I'll be real good the way I should and nevermore make war
>   CHORUS (twice)

. . . too young to bury . . .   *Irv LeVine*

They take a boy out of his natural habitat and teach him to fire a gun, march and be confused along with a whole lot of others just like him. But, they can't take the wonder for life that lives in all such young men. Combat! Girls! Mom's Apple Pie! All of these revolve around him in a swirl of activity. Then you add shooting, diving, ducking, and a natural "I WANNA GO HOME" theme begins to grow in his head. This song takes the listener through a quick trip from boot camp to the lad's first male-female encounter and through the confusion of his first night fire fight. He's a man and he sticks with his outfit and his buddies. But there is always the urge to finish his hitch, get on that Freedom Bird, and GO HOME. Naive he may be; but the lad ain't dumb.

Photo courtesy of Paul Lunsway

LAVC2

Wow! Jeeps have sure come a long way!

710   Robin Olds, All-American Boy

There is an American fighting man, Robin Olds is his true name
He started life in the Hawaiian Isles, his flying brought him fame
He was his father's oldest son, his mother's pride and joy
And dearly did his country love this All-American boy

His schooling took him to West Point, to flight school and beyond
When World War Two beckoned to him, he quickly
      crossed the pond
He flew the Lightning far and fast, he did so with esprit
And soon the Luftwaffe knew his name; for a double ace was he

When the war was over, over there, they gave him
      stateside command
The Korean conflict was building fast in that far off Asian land
He flew a Sabre, he worked a desk, he did both with great class
Since they would not let him fly and fight; his foe became the brass

Then they needed him in Vietnam to lead, fly and fight once more
In yet another far off land on another foreign shore
The Ubon Pack became his gang, the Phantom Two his steed
And history notes and here I quote, "he answered every need"

He shot down many Russian MiGs, they only counted four
He only left when his job was done, and he walked through
      history's door
There are those that do not remember him, this manly
      man 'mongst men

But his Wolfpack gang they all recall and would follow him again

There's more to tell for he's not gone, not vanished in the night

His words still echo loud and clear:

"Peace is not my profession — my profession is to fly and fight!"

... All-American Boy ...   *Irv LeVine*

Robin Olds is a fighter pilot's pilot. He's been there, done that and has come home to tell about it. He's fought the enemy in two wars and at times he had to fight the bullheaded thinking of the brass. He was never known to duck a fight and never known to take a lot of shit from anyone.

A man among men is to be admired and followed and the men under his command were only too willing to go where he led them. I think the words of this song tell it like it is and was. A little speculation in some areas, perhaps, and a bit of hero worship in others tells the listener that Robin is a man of his time, a man to be reckoned with, and a leader that men were more than willing to follow into the skies of hell known as North Vietnam.

Scat 27
Robin's Phantom

711   The Chief

It was six decades ago that he was born
He was meant to wear a uniform
Norm Holler was his name, Wisconsin ain't the same
Since the day the sun lit up that glorious morn

He grew up and struck out on his own
To see what lay beyond the gates of home
He climbed up on his scooter, drove it down to the Air Force recruiter
They signed him up and soon ol' Norm was gone

They told him, "You look like a radar man
Go to school and learn the best you can.
Ain't much you need to know, just tell them pilots where to go
And keep the situation well in hand."

He took his radar scope to Vietna
Tto help 'em fight the war and get it won
His boss said, "There's restrictions!" but he flew one combat mission
And dang near lost a stripe for what he'd done

He learned his way around a radar van
Airman Holler's skills were in demand
Northeast Asia he did go; met a girl named Nobuko
His good luck for air-defending in Japan

He traveled north and south and east and west
Germany, Alaska, and all the rest
Pulled a tour at Cheyenne Base keeping track of what's in space

He's the only space junky I have met

He went all the way to E-9 from E-1, for him and Nobuko life's
        been fun
He pulled graveyards, days, and mids; gave it up for helping kids
And the world's a better place for what he's done

The drill team, the military ball; he taught 'em being proud and
        standing tall
Shared their joy and their grief, here's a toast to the Chief
He is the very best that's in us all

. . . just tell them pilots where to go . . .   *Dick Jonas*
  Norm Holler was my first partner as an AFJROTC
instructor at Cactus High School in Glendale, Arizona. He is
among the very finest NCOs I've ever worked with. A powerful
mentor, he taught me how to empathize with and effectively
instruct teenagers. He taught me how to use the computer, an
Apple IIE with 128 kb of RAM. I owe the Chief a lot.

The Cactus Cobras
Junior ROTC is good for kids.

712   Warrior Bards

All across the countryside you'll hear them sing and play
Those warrior bards from long ago; oh, it seems like yesterday
They'll sing you songs of fighting men on land and in the sky
Of how it felt to live back then and to have their good friends die
BLUE YODEL CHORUS

They tried to put the screws to Toby Hughes up at old Tchepone
Chip Dockery sings harmony even when he's all alone
Jonathan he flew the O-1E without a bloomin' care
Bull Durham's keen for a Jolly Green, and Dick's been everywhere
BLUE YODEL CHORUS

Chuck Rosenberg needs a friendly FAC, and he's searchin'
high and low
Why Broudy sings of green T-shirts, well, it's something I don't know
There's the High Priced Help, Bill Ellis, too, and yodeling Irv LeVine
They're all a part — and they sing from the heart — of that yesterday
and time
BLUE YODEL CHORUS

Now, that Agent Orange, it killed the trees; bullets killed the men
So many faces, so many places, well, I can't say where or when
LBJ, he passed away; McNamara took a fall
And more than 58,000 names got etched on a coal black wall
BLUE YODEL CHORUS

Yes, all across the countryside you'll hear them sing and play
Those warrior bards from long ago, oh, it seems like yesterday

LBJ, he passed away; McNamara took a fall

And more than 58,000 names got etched on a coal black wall

BLUE YODEL CHORUS

Warrior Bards *Irv LeVine*

Some songs are really difficult to get a hold of to write. This one was easy. My recipe was to take an old Jimmy Rodgers yodel tune, add the guys that were most visible on my horizon and then tell their story with a bit of my own and some history thrown in. It is my tribute to all the Warrior Bards who sang to others, or just to themselves — some of whom didn't come home and whose voices won't be heard again. They should be remembered, and I tried to do that with this simple song. This one practically wrote itself . . . or were there other hands on my pen helping me out . . . ?

Photo by Kelly Soldwedel

A Random Warrior Bard

They look at their chording fingers a lot, and screw up their faces funny when they sing.

7-26

713   Kansas Flash

Home folks think I'm big in Taichung city
From the letters that I write they think I'm great
I tell them of the fun I've had in old Taichung
I sign my name with love to Kansas State

I'm gonna go fly, gonna go fly; oh lord, I'm gonna go fly

Next day I went to fly in Charlie Kilo
I launched myself out on an AHC
I had my shit together in fair and stormy weather
The 18th Wing honcho was flying with me

I better watch out, I better watch out; oh lord, I gotta watch out

I found myself adrift out on the ocean
In a little rubber dinghy three feet long
I thought that I'd done right, but halfway through the night
I realized I really had done wrong

I had to punch out, I had to punch out; oh lord, I had to punch out

The first thing that I saw was Ooze 47
He launched himself from out of CCK
He weren't hauling trash and you can bet your ass
Thanks to him I'll see the light of day

I wanta go home, I wanta go home; oh lord, I wanta go home

Then I got the word from Colonel Whiskey

"I got a C-130 on the scene

The weather sure is fine, the moon is gonna shine

I'm gonna bring you home in a Jolly Green."

I wanta go home, I wanta go home; oh lord, I wanta go home

Just sump'n 'bout Kansas   *Dick Jonas*

I think it might be magic. Every pilot I ever knew who came from Kansas had golden hands. Al Smith, an OV-10 jock I transitioned to the Phantom; Dickie Myers, who served four years as JCS Chairman; and Ron Keys, who recently took over at Air Combat Command, boss of all USAF combat planes in the USA.

This yarn is about Ron. Joe Philip named him "Puppy." We were TDY from Kadena Air Base Okinawa, at CCK (Ching Chuan Kang) Air Base Taiwan. A graduate of the Fighter Weapons School at Nellis, and a wing IP, Ron goes out one day to take the Wingco on an AHC (Aircraft Handling Characteristics) training mission. They're single ship and the training area is Charlie Kilo, over the East China Sea. That day, I was the SOF (Supervisor of Flying - the DCO's 'man on the scene'.) After they'd been gone a couple of hours, I go out on the ramp to see if they're back yet. They aren't, so I head for the Command Post, and run into my boss, Bill Weiger. "Jonas! Where's the wing commander!?" Bill was never one to mince words. "I'm checking on that right now, Sir," is my reply.

The CP starts a search. Nobody has seen nor heard from them since they left. We were guests of the 374th Airlift Wing, and they were kind enough to send a flock of C-130's out to hunt for them. Ooze 47 found them — ". . . adrift out on the ocean, in a little rubber dinghy . . . " They called in a Jolly Green from Kadena, who picked them up and took them to the Navy hospital in Taipei. Both guys were okay, just a bit water-logged.

Next day, we greet the returning prodigals with this song.

Turns out, the guy in front put the airplane in a spin. Ron takes over and gets an *aerodynamic* recovery — didn't have to use the drag chute. See? Golden hands.

Just as the rotation stops, the guy up front stuffs in a whole shit-load of opposite rudder, and Big Ugly wraps back up in the opposite direction. By now they're down to punch out altitude, so they hit the silk.

The rest is history — or, legend, perhaps. Ron's a 4-star now and still the pride and joy of Kansas State. He's known now as "Yoda," and I think I know why.

714 Yodel-de-O

I went across to Switzerland
To find a girl; I was a lonely man
I found her there; gave her a kiss
We sing together; it sounds like this

CHORUS

Yodel-de-O, yodel-de-O, yodel-de-O, yodel-de-O
Yodel-de-O, yodel-de-O, yodel-de-odel-de-odel-de-odel-de-O

I married her; we settled down
In a little brown house close to town
We had some kids; oh, two or three
And now they sing with her and me

CHORUS

Her dad made cheese — the kind called Swiss
Our love gave us perfect bliss
But singing or eating that old Swiss cheese
The sounds we made came out like these

CHORUS

(. . . yodel finale . . .)

The Yodeler *Irv LeVine*

I wrote this sing-along yodel song back in 1956 and it has been a favorite with audiences around the world. It gives them a chance to yodel and to laugh at themselves and the experience of being a part of the fun. Listening is great, but participation takes a front seat. Yodeling is sort of my logo. My daddy always said, "If you can't sing good, sing LOUD." And any one who's heard me

Sound of Music?

Not exactly von Trapp, but close enough!

(Irv at happy hour, Leeuwarden O'Club, RNLAF, 13 June 2003.)

8

Dick Jonas

Bull Durham

Toby Hughes

Boozin' Buddies

Irv LeVine

EROSONIC   Album Eight

Dick Jonas flew 125 F-4 combat missions in the Vietnam War. He served twice in the 8th Fighter Wing Wolfpack, in Thailand and the Republic of Korea. He retired from the Air Force in 1986 as a Lieutenant Colonel. He holds three Distinguished Flying Crosses and 13 Air Medals.

Lieutenant Colonel James Patterson Durham — Bull — is a veteran of Korea and Vietnam. He flew the B-29, B-36, B-52, and EC/AC-47. He holds the Distinguished Flying Cross and the Air Medal.

Lieutenant Colonel William F. (Toby) Hughes was an F-4 Phantom pilot, flying the Ho Chi Minh Trail and elsewhere on 204 missions in the Vietnam War. He holds the Silver Star, the Distinguished Flying Cross and 10 Air Medals.

Major Irv LeVine flew the F-105 Thunderchief out of Korat, Thailand on 100 missions over North Vietnam. He holds the Silver Star, 3 Distinguished Flying Crosses and 16 Air Medals.

8 0 1   Boozin' Buddies

Author unknown; Air Force traditional. From a jam session with Toby Hughes and Chip Dockery. Arr ©2002 Dick Jonas. All rights reserved.

CHORUS
We are the boys who fly high in the sky, bosom buddies while
boozin' are we
We are the boys who they send up to die, bosom buddies while
boozin' are we
Up in headquarters they scream and they shout
Talkin' bout things they know nothing about
We are the boys who they send up to die, bosom buddies while
boozin' are we

We stand 'neath silent rafters, the walls around us are bare
They echo back our laughter, it seems that the dead are still there
So, stand to your glasses steady, let not a tear fill your eye
A toast to the dead already, hoorah for the next man to die
CHORUS

In flaming Spad and Camel, with wings of wood and steel
For mortal stakes we gamble with cards that are stacked for the deal
Stand to your glasses steady, let not a tear . . .
CHORUS

Denied by the land that bore us, betrayed by the ones we hold dear
The good have all gone before us and only the dull are still here
Stand to your glasses steady, let not a tear . . .
CHORUS

We climb in the purple twilight, we loop in the silvery dawn

Black smoke trails behind us to show where our comrades

> have gone

> > Stand to your glasses steady, let not a tear . . .
> > CHORUS

. . . We are the boys . . .   *Dick Jonas*
        . . . and the girls, too. That's Bessie Coleman in the
driver's seat of the Jenny. She was the first black (actually,
Cherokee blood from her father's side of the family also flowed in
her veins) woman to obtain a flying license — from the Federa-
tion Aeronautique Internationale (FAI), in France. She was born
in Texas in 1892, learned to fly in 1921, and died in an aircraft
accident in 1926. I have no doubt that had our society been as
progressive a century ago as it is today, she would have flown in
the same battles as Rickenbacker, Luke, and the Red Baron.
Girls do fly air combat today — check CD Album #12 "Passing
the Flame."

Curtiss JN-4 Jenny
WWI U. S. trainer

802 Yay-Boo

Good afternoon. I've got a few things to say to you this afternoon, and I want you to know — at any time if you have an input . . . I appreciate it. You know how much I appreciate your input . . .

Now when I take over this place there's gonna be some changes
made — **BOO**
Some *drastic* changes — **YAY**

We're gonna burn the place down — **BOO**
But we'll build a *new* one — **YAY**

The bar's gonna be a foot wide — **BOO**
And one mile long — **YAY**

There'll be no bartenders — **BOO**
They'll all be *barmaids* — **YAY**

All the barmaids are gonna be dressed — **BOO**
. . . In *Saran Wrap* — **YAY**

You can't take our barmaids home — **BOO**
They take *you* home — **YAY**

You can't sleep with the barmaids — **BOO**
They won't *let* you sleep — **YAY**

No women allowed in the front part of the bar — **BOO**
With *clothes* on — **YAY**

There'll be no loving on the dancing floor — **BOO**
There'll be no *dancing* on the *loving* floor — **YAY**

Front door closes at midnight — **BOO**
Back door opens at *12:01* — **YAY**

Beer is five dollars a glass — **BOO**
Whiskey is f*ree* — **YAY**

Only one drink to a customer — **BOO**
Served in *buckets* — **YAY**

We're gonna throw all the beer in the river — **BOO**
Then we'll all go *swimming* — **YAY**

Parties make the world go 'round, world go 'round, world go 'round
Parties make the world go 'round, let's have a party

Colonel Bull   *Irv LeVine*
        This narrative-song is a classic. None better to lead it
than the old soldier/airman, James "Bull" Durham. Bull is gone
now, but his legacy in story and song lives on. He'd do this bit of
tongue-in-cheek entertainment with a twinkle in his eye that told
you it was more fact than fiction as far as he was
concerned. Believe me, if they had thrown all the booze in the
river, Bull would have been the first one in. The narrative tells
the story of the upper echelons not understanding the needs of
the grunts. Bull understood better than anyone I ever knew.

803 Airman's Toast

Air Force traditional. Arrangement and music ©2002 by Dick Jonas. All rights reserved.

Here's to me in my sober mood
When I ramble, sit, and think
And here's to me in my drunken mood
When I gamble, sin, and drink

When my flying days are over
And from this life I pass
I hope they bury me upside down
So the world can kiss my ass

(. . . instrumental break . . .)

Here's to me in my sober mood
When I ramble, sit, and think
And here's to me in my drunken mood
When I gamble, sin, and drink

When my flying days are over
And from this life I pass
I hope they bury me upside down
So the world can kiss my ass

. . . upside down . . .   *Dick Jonas*

A rarity for most fighter pilots, the tune to this toast is original with me. I had heard the toast repeated many times in stag bars and at parties. I thought it would stick with me better if it had a tune. The thought is typical. Fighter pilots are not happy unless they get to go upside down at least once on each sortie. They regularly thumb their noses at the rest of society and the world. The words "kiss my ass" leap so readily to their lips.

Actually, I view that as an asset. It means they will stand their ground until they draw the last breath. They will NOT permit the enemy to cross the line. Come to think of it, not just fighter pilots, but most of the truly professional warriors I have known all felt the same way — rifle toters, tankers, boat drivers — they're all alike. America is safe thereby.

P-40

Republic of China livery

804   Golden Jock Strap

Oh, my golden jock hangs on the wall
In a place of honor just down the hall
Couldn't cover my ass, but it saved my balls
When I rode in the Thud in the morning

      CHORUS
      Oh that golden jock strap! Oh, that golden jock strap
      The golden jock I always wore, 'cause it fit so neat
      Oh that golden jock strap! Oh, that golden jock strap
      The golden jock I always wore, and I don't mean on my feet

It's the same old jock that I wore aloft
Yours may be brass but mine are soft
And I didn't want Ho to shoot 'em off
When I rode in the Thud in the morning
      CHORUS

Now, some will call us silly fools
We fought and flew by golden rules
Golden jocks were basic tools
And they help protect our family jewels
      CHORUS

If you were a jock with lots of sass
And didn't wanta get one up your ass
You wore a jock which added class
When you flew in your Thud in the morning
      CHORUS

When you go to Heaven, now, don't be late

Just fly your Thud through Pete's front gate

You're the guy he won't try to stop

He'll know you by your golden jock

CHORUS

. . . by your golden jock . . .   *Irv LeVine*

  I first wrote this while serving at Korat. Everyone knew about "The Golden BB" — the one that could get you no matter what you did to prevent it. Fighter pilots are a curious mixture of guts and superstition. They'll charge Hell with a bucket of water but are loath to walk under a ladder or let a black cat cross their path before a mission. So, what could be better than a golden jock strap to ward off incoming? It didn't much cover anyone's ass but it sure helped to keep the family jewels for future genera-tions. I changed the verses a bit for this CD in order to protect the weenies that were the members of the other squadrons. Friendly rivalry? My ass. The Golden Jock must have worked. I went Downtown 42 times without a scratch. So you can see, it worked for me . . .

www.aviation-art.net/

F-105

. . . saved my balls . . .

Special thanks to Lou Drendel for the Thud pic.

805 Benny Havens, Oh

Come fill your glasses, fellows, and stand up in a row
To singing sentimentally, we're going for to go
In the Army there's sobriety, promotions very slow
So we'll sing our reminiscences of Benny Haven's, Oh!

CHORUS

Oh! Benny Haven's, Oh! Oh, Benny Haven's, Oh!
We'll sing our reminiscences of Benny Haven's, Oh!

Of the lovely maids with virgin lips, like roses dipped in dew
Who are to be our better halves, we'd like to take a view
But sufficient to the bridal day is the ill of it, you know
So we'll cheer our hearts with chorusing at Benny Haven's, Oh!

Now, another star has faded, we miss its brilliant glow
Another friend has ceased to be a soldier here below
And the country which he honored now feels a heartfelt woe
As we toast his name in reverence at Benny Haven's, Oh!

CHORUS

When this life's troubled sea is o'er, and our last battle's through
If God permits us mortals then his blest domain to view
Then shall we see with glory crowned, in proud celestial row
The friends we've known and loved so well at Benny Haven's, Oh!

May the Army be augmented, promotion be less slow

May our country in the hour of need be ready for the foe

May we find a soldier's resting-place beneath a soldier's blow

With space enough beside our graves for Benny Haven's, Oh!

CHORUS

. . . space enough . . . *Dick Jonas*

The most popular, and oldest, of all West Point Songs still being sung is "Benny Havens, Oh!." Benny Havens himself was a very real person about whom many traditions have entwined themselves. Benny was here [at West Point] on and off in many capacities from 1804 to 1812, returning permanently in the early 1820's. He opened a small tavern and his business was so flourishing that the Superintendent barred him from the reservation. Benny then opened a slightly larger establishment in Highland Falls and it was here that the song "Benny Havens, Oh!" was born. Under the influence of Benny's famous flip, Lieutenant O'Brien composed the first few stanzas of this song to the tune of "The Wearin' o' the Green." Anecdotes concerning Benny's tavern are numberless and became tradition when Benny passed away in 1877. Innumerable stanzas have been added to the song.

(From the *1957 Bugle Notes of the United States Corps of Cadets* U. S. Military Academy, West Point.)

806   Peacemaker

I am a SAC weenie, I have lots of fun
I am a peace-lovin' son-of-a-gun
I spend all my flight pay on women and booze
And fly this big bastard wherever I choose
> I left my old homeplace way down on the farm
> Signed up with the Air Force to mother's alarm
> With a bar on my collar and a yoke in my hand
> This was my way of becoming a man

She ain't no machbuster, this bastard's too big
Too many motors, she flies like a pig
Takes an interstate highway to get off the ground
But I'll admit that I love her when no one's around
> This harlot stays airborne for nearly a week
> I eat here, I sleep here, at 40,000 feet
> A bathroom and shower are some of her tricks
> Two things you can't get in an F-86

They call her Peacemaker, she's a beautiful thing
Five big ass motors hung on each wing
Pistons and turbines is what makes her run
You bet your ass, bro, she gets the job done
> She totes a big bomb load for 10,000 miles
> Up front on the panel is an acre of dials
> Now, I fly the left seat; I'd do it for free
> At last, I'm the boss of this big essobee

She goes on forever and there's nothing to fix
Just ain't no bomber like a B-36
Someday I will leave her, then what will I do?
I'll park my young ass in a B-52!

Bull Durham *Dick Jonas*

When we were cooking up this album, Bull confided to me that he didn't have any songs to contribute to the effort. But, I wanted him on it, so I told him I'd write a couple for him. *Peacemaker* was one of them.

Bull flew all the big ones — the B-29, the B-36, and the B-52. I should have questioned a long time ago how a bomber puke could hold his own so well with a bunch of fighter pogues. But he could do that. There was just one of him and upwards of a half-dozen of us, but he was never outnumbered. On stage, he was more flamboyant than we were. He was funnier than us, too; he could keep them rolling in the aisles when he wanted to.

He looked a bit like Colonel Sanders (KFC) with his van Dyke whiskers. He was tall — over six feet, I think — and he towered well above my five-and-a-half feet. He used to drape his arm across my shoulders, lean down into my face and say, "Dick, we're gonna be fartin' through silk, and wearin' diamonds big as horse turds!" He was so convincing.

Bull did write a bunch of his own songs, about life in SAC (LeMay's bomber command.) His *Songs of SAC/SEA* album is one of my favorites. He did equally as good a job of musically portraying the plight of the poor bomber pilot as any of us ever did for the hot rock fighter jock.

I'm sure that Heaven is somewhat different, now that Bull Durham is there.

B-36 Peacemaker

. . . a *big* bomb load . . .

8-14

807   Roll Your Leg Over

Air Force Traditional. Arrangement ©2002 Dick Jonas. All rights reserved.

Roll your leg over, oh, roll your leg over
>Roll your leg over it's better that way

If all little girls were like fish in the ocean
And I were a whale I would teach them emotion
>Roll your leg over, oh, roll your leg over
>Roll your leg over the Man in the Moon

If all little girls were like fish in the river
>And I were a sand bar, I'd sure make them quiver, roll your . . .

If all little girls were like bells in the tower
>And I were a clapper, I'd bang by the hour, roll your leg . . .

If all little girls were like bats in a steeple
>And I were a bat, there'd be more bats than people, roll . . .

If all little girls were like little white rabbits
>And I were a hare, I would teach them bad habits, roll . . .

If all little girls were like Hedy LaMarr
>I'd try twice as hard and get twice as far, roll your leg over . . .

If all little girls were like Gypsy Rose Lee
>And I were a g-string, oh boy, what I'd see! roll your leg . . .

If all little girls were like nurses who would
>And I were a doctor, I would if I could, roll your leg over . . .

I wish little girls were like bricks in a pile
>And I were a mason, I'd lay them in style, roll your leg over . . .

I wish little girls were like statues of Venus
>And I were a man with a petrified penis, roll your leg over . . .

*

I wish little girls were like mountain road passes
And I were a sports car I'd buzz all their asses, roll your leg over . . .

I wish little girls were like diamonds and rubies
And I were a jeweler, I'd polish their boobies, roll your leg over . . .

**

I wish little girls were like B-29's
And I flew a fighter, I'd buzz their behinds, roll your leg over . . .

> Roll your leg over, oh, roll your leg over
> Roll your leg over it's better that way
>
> Roll your leg over, oh, roll your leg over
> Roll your leg over the Man in the Moon

. . . the Man in the Moon . . .   *Dick Jonas*
    Without a doubt, these are not the only verses to this anthem which have been, or will be, concocted by creative warriors everywhere. As a matter of fact, I, myself, have thought of a couple more since we recorded the song. I choose to insert them at the single and double asterisks above:

*   *I think little girls are like strawberry pie*
    I don't know the reason so don't ask me why, roll your leg over . . .

**   *Oh! I thought of the reason for strawberry pie*
    It tastes 'bout as good as p-u-s-s-y, roll your leg over . . .

808   Buff

This old girl's a half a century old
She flies way up where the air is cold
You bet it's gonna be tuff, if you're underneath my Buff
And may God have mercy on your soul

She sets there cold and dark and all alone
I just hope they never ring that phone
'Cause if they do I'll puke six or seven great big nukes
In the back yard of someone else's home

She hauls a hundred plus Mark 82's
And when she flies I mind my P's and Q's
I've flown this big ass Bongo from Beale to the Congo
Routine for a B-52

I flew the Arc Lights over Vietnam
I did it all for my Uncle Sam
I heard 'em weep and wail up and down the Ho Chi Trail
Fuck the bastards; I don't give a damn

They sent for me in 1991
I told myself, "Now this is gonna be fun!"
They called it "Desert Storm," and I made it mighty warm
For them essobees beneath the desert sun

Bin Laden and the Al Qaeda, too
Found out what the mighty Buff can do
She beat the Taliban all around Afghanistan
Until their bloody ass was black and blue

She's been around since Jesus was a boy
Ain't no place in this world she can't deploy
She's johnny-on-the spot whenever things get hot
I thank the USA for my big toy

Big Ugly Fat Fucker   *Dick Jonas*
        . . . or, Big Ugly Fat Fellow if you're in mixed company.
We called the A-7 the "SLUF" and it worked the same way. The
BUFF is perhaps the shrewdest investment the American tax-
payer ever made. Same with the T-38. Both machines have been
around for about a half-century.
        I'll never forget watching an Arc Light drop. We were on
our way back to Ubon and the AC had given me the stick. I was
mesmerized by the huge formation of bombers off in the distance
and was not paying enough attention to my navigation. "Don't fly
under them!" the AC exclaimed. In the years since, I've figured
out why.

B-52 Stratofortress
The mighty BUFF

809   Hey, Mr Taliban (AAAAAAAYO! AAAAAAYO!)

HAAAAAAAYO! HAAAAAAYO!
>   Air Force come, gonna flatten your home

First, World War Two and then Korea
Air Force come gonna flatten your home
Then Vietnam and now diarrhea
Air Force come, gonna flatten your home

>   CHORUS

>>   Hey! Mr. Taliban we know where you're hiding
>>   Air Force come gonna flatten your home
>>   Hey! Mr. Taliban we know where you're hiding
>>   Air Force come, gonna flatten your home

The stealth fighter come, mon, you ain't gon' see it
Air Force come gonna flatten your home
Then B-52's, mon, you ain' gon' believe it
Air Force come, gonna flatten your home

A sixty foot, seventy foot, eighty foot crater
Air Force come gonna flatten your home
Uncle Sam's pissed, mon, he ain' no Quaker
Air Force come, gonna flatten your home

>   CHORUS

When we done you all be cryin'

Air Force come gonna flatten your home

The pilots are brothers of the New York firemen

Air Force come, gonna flatten your home

AAAAAY U.S.A., U.S.A. U.S.AAAAY-O

Air Force come, gonna flatten your home

...advice...   *Irv LeVine*

When *Aaaaaaaayo* is sung for a mixed group of pilots and wives, the jocks give it their all, but the wives breathe fire into the chorus — " . . . **AIR FORCE COME GONNA FLATTEN YOUR HOME** . . . "

No wonder so many planes are named after wives and sweethearts, those outstanding members of the opposite, and supposedly weaker, sex.

Today's advice is, "Hey Mr Taliban, better CYA . . . "

F-117 Nighthawks

Actually, they're not really there. It's the nature of stealth.

810   The Last Fighter Pilot

He was born in the skies over France back in 1916
A daring young man in a flimsy old flying machine
Ed Rickenbacker, the Baron, Frank Luke and the rest
Paving the high road for those who would follow the quest

    In the 20's and 30's he stood against short-sighted men
    Who clipped back his wings, saying they'll never need him again

Then he strapped on a Spitfire and climbed through the bright
    English blue
To the cheers of the many who owed so much to the few
From the white cliffs of Dover to islands of jungle and sand
A whole world at war, but for him it was man against man

    And when it was over he stood against short-sighted men
    Who clipped back his wings, saying they'll never need him again

Then he climbed in a Sabre and flew through the Korean sky
Up to MiG Alley, with courage to fight and to die
And in Southeast Asia he called down the thunder again
But this one was different; they wouldn't allow him to win

    And when it was over he listened to short-sighted men
    Who said it was his fault, and they'd never need him again

The last fighter pilot is just like the first of his kind

And when duty calls he's the first to step over the line

A child of the heavens, a grandson and son of the best

Still riding the high road and trying to follow the quest

In the twenty-first century he stands against short-sighted men

Who'll clip back his wings when they think they don't need

him again

For you self-serving bastards who kill with the stroke of a pen

He stands at the ready — for the day that you need him again

The High Road   *Toby Hughes*
From *What The Captain Means: A Song of the In-Country Air War*
©2005 William F. "Toby" Hughes

Whatever you've heard about the Vietnam war, whatever you believe, also believe this: Those who fought in the skies of Southeast Asia did so in the finest tradition of the American Fighting Man. They gave substance to the credo, "Duty well-performed; Honor in all things; Country above self." There was little personal glory in this one, and they knew it. Yet from Ca Mau, on the tip of the Mekong Delta, to Thai Nguyen and the hell-filled skies over Hanoi, they faced death on a daily basis. In thankless effort they carried the war to the enemy more than a million times, with the passing of time recorded in missions flown and the cost recorded in friends left behind. Yet despite these things, despite vilification from their own countrymen, despite comic opera restraints that decreed that the war could be fought only on the enemy's terms, despite defenses unmatched in the history of war in the air, they flew and fought. And they almost pulled it off. The world will never know, nor does it want to hear, how they had victory in their grasp, only to have it traded away in one final concession by those to whom the politically expedient is the way, the truth and the light. Only *they* know, and they will keep that knowledge with them to their final breaths. Their courage, loyalty, professionalism and patriotism are a matter of record, and are never to be questioned *by anyone!*

And as the call has come, and will again, from the Book of Isaiah, "Whom shall I send, and who will go for us?", those who follow the high quest will answer as they always have:

"Here am I; send me."

8 1 1   Reunion

Faces in a book of faded pictures
Model planes upon the dusty shelves
Memories of the time they rode the thunder
Part of something bigger than themselves

      A time when great machines took wing in anger
      When strong men set their skills against the foe
      In deadly rains of fire and skies of danger
      Like none who were not part of it can know

The roll is long in valor's Hall of Honor
And many fell on far-off foreign sod
We cherish those who rest in honored glory
And those whose fate is known but to their God

      They bravely rose to heed the call of duty
      They lived with honor, and in honor died
      Standing in their country's time of trial
      To try and stem the dark oppressing tide

Ten thousand miles from home and hearth and loved ones
Living in a world they never made
Brothers in a time of blood and dying
A comradeship with bonds that never fade

      So here's to Thud and Phantom and Skyraider
      And here's to Bird Dog, Jolly Green and Hun
      To the men who flew the skies of Southeast Asia
      And those friends of ours who flew too near the sun

Let's remember all the friends who've gone before us
Let's remember both the good times and the scars
We'll all meet at that final great reunion
And fly with angels out beyond the stars

Let's remember all the friends who've gone before us
Let's remember both the good times and the scars
We'll all meet at that final great reunion
And fly with angels out beyond the stars
We'll all meet at that final great reunion
And we'll fly with angels out beyond the stars

. . . And fly with angels . . .   *Toby Hughes*
From *What The Captain Means: A Song of the In-Country Air War*
©2005 William F. "Toby" Hughes
     This song is dedicated to men with whom I once shared the sky, forty-six Air Force pilots, all now memories and names on a wall. They were squadron-mates and others with whom I shared a drink or a dice game or a war story or an arm-wrestle or a fistfight or a song around the bar. They were my teachers and my students, my leaders and my wingmen. Some were friends; some were not. But all were part of the worldwide fraternity of men who fly and fight, one of the closest-knit groups on the planet. They accepted the risks of what they were asked to do, giving or asking no special favors, no quarter.
     In the classic musical play "Carousel" it is said that a person lives on, so long as there is one on earth who remembers. To those we knew, now on the Wall, and to the more than fifty-eight thousand others there with them, let us dedicate our efforts to ensuring that they indeed live on for as long as this nation remains worthy of their sacrifice. And let us also work to ensure that as later generations, present and future, are called upon to heed the call of Mars, they are better prepared than we were, better supported on the home front than we were, and most important of all, that they are allowed, as we were denied, the opportunity to do the job right.
     To those who went, to those who came home, to those who didn't, to those who haven't yet.

8 1 2   I Don't Want To Join The Army

I don't want to join the Army, I don't want to go to war
I'd rather hang around Picadilly Underground
Living off the earnings of a high class lady
I don't want a bullet up me arse hole
Don't want me buttocks shot away
I'd rather stay in England, jolly, jolly England
And fornicate me bloody life away
       . . . gor blimey . . .

Monday I touched her on the ankle
Tuesday I touched her on the knee
Wednesday with success I lifted up her dress
Thursday, her chemise, gor blimey . . .
Friday I put me hand upon it
Saturday night she gave me balls a tweak — tweak! tweak!
Sunday after supper, I shoved the old boy up her
And now she's making seven bob a week
       . . . gor blimey . . .

I don't want to join the Army, I don't want to go to war
I'd rather hang around Picadilly Underground
Living off the earnings of a high class lady
I don't want a bullet up me arse hole
Don't want me buttocks shot away
I'd rather stay in England, jolly, jolly England
And fornicate me bloody life away

. . . gor blimey . . .   *Dick Jonas*

I had been able to sing the first and last (which is the same as the first) stanzas of this thing for decades. I never got the Monday through Sunday stuff squared away until I decided to record it on this album. I found out it wasn't so hard to do, after all.

I suspect lurking in the dark labyrinths of the warriors heart, is the secret desire to sit out the war in Picadilly Underground, or wherever serves that purpose. I confess, I really did not want my " . . . buttocks shot away . . . " in Vietnam. If I'd had my 'druthers, I would have sat it out down in northern Florida along the banks of the Suwannee River where I grew up. That is, after I had some first hand experience with getting shot at. I did not feel that way at first.

I had wanted to be a military flyer since boyhood. Work in the field on my daddy's northern Florida one-horse farm was frequently interrupted by overflying fighter planes from NAS Jacksonville and Cecil Field. As I approached graduation from college (Valdosta State, in south Georgia) the prospect of realizing that dream became palpable. I couldn't wait. I was so afraid the Vietnam fracas would be over before I could get a piece of it.

Eighteen months later, after pilot training and combat crew training in the F-4, I found myself in the pipeline to Southeast Asia. Now I was afraid it was *not* going to be over before I found myself in the middle of it. People were getting shot down and killed or taken prisoner. Not exactly what I had projected for myself.

Well; the bottom line is, God was good to me. I never took a scratch, though I did come close a time or two. When I had flown the last one, I hove a huge sigh of relief and thankfully boarded the freedom bird.

According to my bud, Irv LeVine, *gor blimey* is of London origin and is a phonetic corruption of "God blind me," a fairly old fashioned oath.

813　Wake Island

TIME! Our country needed time! Political correctness wasn't an option back then. If they heard anyone calling them heroes, the men of that time would have laughed in their faces. They were simply Americans doing what was necessary in the face of overwhelming odds. This handful of men was willing to sacrifice themselves on the altar of freedom. Wake Island, December 8th, 1941, withstood 19 consecutive bombings and dozens of shellings before running out of supplies and equipment to continue the resistance.

December the 7th they heard about Pearl
They knew they'd be next on the list
450, no more, those brave men all swore
To fight to the death, to resist

> CHORUS
> Wake Island (Wake Island) Wake Island (Wake Island)
> It wasn't yet marked on the map
> Those men raised her name to honor and fame
> When they stopped the advance of the Japs

Cut off from supplies with no hope of aid
They spotted the first Japanese
With thousands of troops and a task force of ships
The Japs thought they'd take them with ease
> CHORUS

They sent in their subs, their ships and their planes
They shelled them by day and by night
"Surrender or die!" They laughed at the threat
Said, "We're only beginning to fight!"
CHORUS

Those 450 stopped 6,000 Japs
Their fighters downed 28 planes
They sank two destroyers and one submarine
And the rest all got shelled for their pains
CHORUS

Their plan was to fight to the very last man
But Devereaux gave this command
There's a thousand civilians we can't sacrifice
And we'll have to surrender our men
CHORUS

They laid down their arms on the twenty-third day
The Japs cheered the news of defeat
But they could not explain how a handful of men
Could stop the whole fucking Jap fleet
CHORUS

Such Men *Irv LeVine*

Where do we get such men? They come from the caldron of Freedom that makes up these United States, where each and every one of us breathes free because of them. Admiral Yamamoto said before Pearl Harbor, "It is a mistake to regard the Americans as luxury-loving and weak. I can tell you, Americans are full of the spirit of justice, fight and adventure . . . Japan cannot beat America. Therefore, she should not fight America."

He was right; and, the men on Wake Island gave them their first lesson in American "justice, fight and adventure."

814 What the Captain Means

By Lieutenant Colonel Joe Kent, Information Officer of the 12th Tac Fighter Wing, Cam Ranh Bay Air Base, South Vietnam. It was recorded in 1967 at Cam Ranh with Lt Col Kent as IO, Col Travis McNeil as the captain, and a 'major from PACAF' as the reporter. Special thanks to Dr Lydia Fish for its use. Archival material courtesy of the Vietnam Veterans Oral History and Folklore Project. <http://faculty.buffalostate.edu/fishlm/folksongs>

The following is an interview with an F-4C pilot of the 12th Tac Fighter Wing at Cam Ranh Bay. It is complete with the captain's comments, along with the press's interpretation of the captain's comments. The captain's view of the war is most significant for all those who served a year here at Cam Ranh, where the sewer meets the sea.

1. Correspondent: Well, Captain, now that you've flown a few missions, what do you think of the F-4C as a combat aircraft?

Captain: It's the best sonovabitchin' airplane in the whole goddam United States Air Force inventory. It's so fuckin' maneuverable you can fly up your own ass with it.

PAO: What the Captain means is that he has found the F-4C highly maneuverable at all altitudes, and he considers it an excellent aircraft for all missions assigned.

2. Correspondent: I suppose, Captain, you've flown a certain number of missions in North Vietnam. What did you think of the SAMs used by the North Vietnamese?

Captain: Why, those bastards couldn't hit a bull in the ass with a bass fiddle. We fake the shit out of them. There's no sweat.

PAO: What the Captain means is that the surface-to-air missiles around Hanoi pose a serious problem to our air operations and that the pilots have a healthy respect for them.

3. Correspondent: I suppose, Captain, that you've flown missions to the South. What kind of ordnance do you use, and what kind of targets do you hit?

Captain: Well, I'll tell you, mostly we aim at kicking the shit out of Vietnamese villages; and my favorite ordnance is napalm. Man, that stuff just sucks the air out of their friggin' lungs and makes a sonovabitchin' fire.

PAO: What the Captain means is that air strikes in South Vietnam are often against Viet Cong structures and all operations are always under the positive control of forward air controllers, or FACs. The ordnance employed is conventional 500- and 750-pound bombs and 20-mm cannon fire.

4. Correspondent: I suppose you spent an R & R in Hong Kong. What were your impressions of the Oriental girls?

Captain: Yeah, I went to Hong Kong. As far as those Oriental broads, well, I don't care which way the runway runs, east or west, north or south — a piece of ass is a piece of ass.

PAO: What the Captain means is that he found the delicately featured Oriental girls fascinating, and he was very impressed with their fine manners and thinks their naivete is most charming.

5. Correspondent: Tell me, Captain, have you flown any missions other than over North and South Vietnam?

Captain: You bet your sweet ass I've flown other missions — missions other than in North and South. We get fragged nearly every day for, uh, over in, uh . . . those fuckers over there throw everything at you but the friggin' kitchen sink. Even the goddamn kids got slingshsots.

PAO: What the Captain means is that he has occasionally been scheduled to fly missions in the extreme western DMZ, and he has a healthy respect for the flak in that area

6. Correspondent: I understand that no one in the 12th Tactical Fighter Wing has got a MiG yet. What seems to be the problem?

Captain: Why you screwhead, if you knew anything about what you're talking about . . . the problem is MiGs. If we'd get fragged by those peckerheads at Seventh for those counters in MiG valley, you can bet your ass we'd get some of them mothers. Those glory hounds at Ubon get all those frags, while we settle for fightin' the friggin' war. Those mothers at Ubon are sitting on their fat asses killing MiGs, and we get stuck with bombing the goddam cabbage patches.

PAO: What the Captain means is that each element of the Seventh Air Force is responsible for doing their assigned job in the air war. Some units are assigned the job of neutralizing enemy air strength by hunting out MiGs, and other elements are assigned bombing missions and interdiction of enemy supply routes.

7. Correspondent: Of all the targets you've hit in Vietnam, which one was the most satisfying?

Captain: Ahh, shit, it was gettin' fragged for that friggin' suspected VC vegetable garden. I dropped napalm in the middle of the fuckin' rutab . . . rutabag . . . and, uh, cabbage, and my wingman splashed it real good with six of those 750-pound mothers and spread the fire all the way to the friggin' beets and carrots.

PAO: What the Captain means is that the great variety of tactical targets available throughout Vietnam make the F-4C the perfect aircraft to provide flexible response.

8. Correspondent: What do you consider the most difficult target you've struck in North Vietnam?

Captain: The friggin' bridges. I must have dropped 40 tons of bombs on those swayin' bamboo mothers, and I ain't hit one of the bastards yet.

8-30.1

PAO: What the Captain means is that interdicting bridges along enemy supply routes is very important and a quite difficult target. The best way to accomplish this task is to crater the approaches to the bridges.

9. Correspondent: I noticed in touring the base that you have aluminum matting on the taxiways. Would you care to comment on its effectiveness and usefulness in Vietnam?

Captain: You fuckin' right I'd like to make a comment. Most of us pilots are well hung, but shit, you don't know what hung is until you get hung up on one of those friggin' bumps on that goddamn stuff.

PAO: What the Captain means is that the aluminum matting is quite satisfactory as a temporary expedient but requires some finesse in taxiing and braking the aircraft.

10. Correspondent: Did you have an opportunity to meet your wife on leave in Honolulu, and did you enjoy the visit with her?

Captain: Yeah, I met my wife in Honolulu, but I forgot to check the calendar, so the whole five days were friggin' well combat- proof — a completely dry run.

PAO: What the Captain means is that it was wonderful to get together with his wife and learn firsthand about the family and how things were at home.

11. Correspondent: Thank you for your time, Captain.

Captain: Screw you; why don't you bastards print the real story, instead of all that crap?

PAO: What the Captain means is that he enjoyed the opportunity to discuss his tour with you.

12. Correspondent: One final question. Could you reduce your impression of the war into a simple phrase or statement, Captain?

Captain: You bet your ass I can. It's a fucked up war.

PAO: What the Captain means is . . . it's a FUCKED UP WAR!

9

God Bless America

EROSONIC
Album Nine

Dick Jonas

Angela Jonas

Angela has been singing since childhood. She remembers singing country and traditional songs with her family. She heeded her mother's advice to take voice lessons and was introduced to the world of opera. She has been performing the music of Puccini, Mozart, and Verdi for 15 years. She studied with Bill Doherty of the Central Florida Lyric Opera, and spent two years in New York City studying and performing. Her most distinguished privilege was being coached in the role of Madama Butterfly by Madame Licia Albanese of the Metropolitan Opera. Madame Albanese is one of the most renowned and respected Butterflys of all time. Angela is back in Orlando, once again singing with the Lyric Opera.

Dick Jonas has been a preacher, a disk jockey, a fighter pilot, an author, an entertainer, and a teacher. He is the father of Angela, Crystal, and Gina, and the grandfather of Christopher, Tyler, Jaclyn, and Cameron.

Lyrics not available.

. . . my home . . .   *Angela Jonas*

This is an audience participation song. It seems that whenever it's sung, the audience automatically joins in. They don't even wait for the performers to give them a signal! And I'm glad of that. Whenever I've performed this hymn I always see many of the people putting their hands on their hearts and rising to their feet in addition to singing along. I only hope that audiences will continue to respond in this way whenever they hear this anthem sung. It gives the folks on stage such a warm feeling.

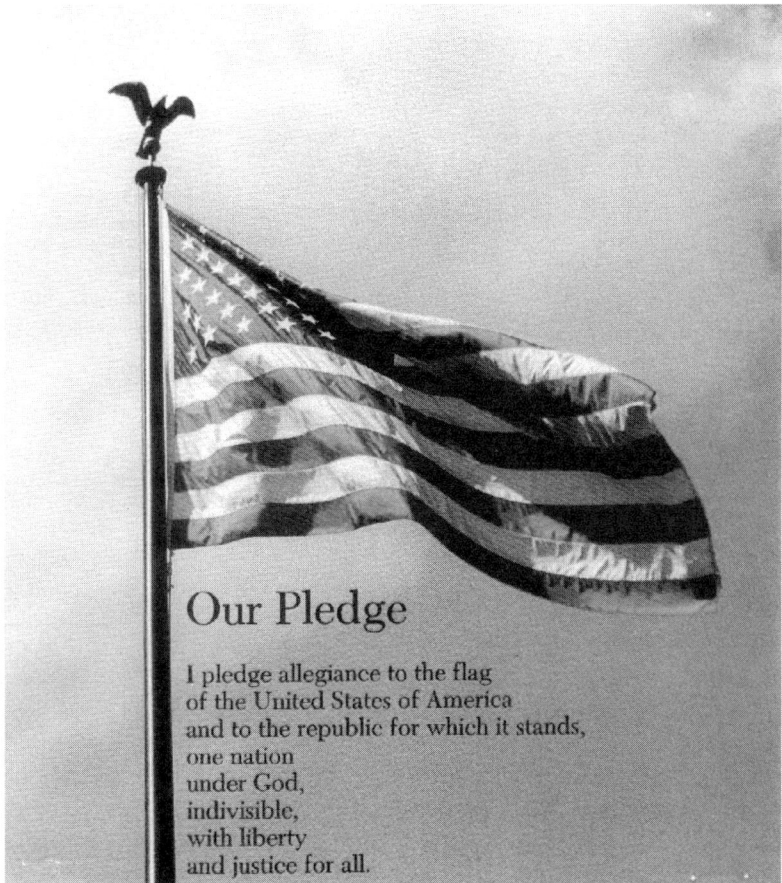

Our Pledge

I pledge allegiance to the flag
of the United States of America
and to the republic for which it stands,
one nation
under God,
indivisible,
with liberty
and justice for all.

902 America the Beautiful/This Land

PD; *This Land Is Your Land* words and music by Woodie Guthrie TRO-©1956 (Renewed) 1970 (Renewed) 1972 (Renewed) Ludlow Music, Inc., New York, NY Used by Permission

Oh, beautiful for spacious skies
For amber waves of grain
For purple mountain majesty above the fruited plain
America, America, God shed His grace on thee
And crown thy good with brotherhood
From sea to shining sea

This land is your land, this land is my land,
From California to the New York Island;
From the redwood forest to the Gulf Stream waters
This land was made for you and me.

As I was walking that ribbon of highway,
I saw above me that endless skyway
I saw below me that golden valley:
This land was made for you and me.

This land is your land, this land is my land,
From California to the New York Island;
From the redwood forest to the Gulf Stream waters
This land was made for you and me.

America, America, God shed His grace on thee
And crown thy good with brotherhood
From sea to shining sea

This land is your land, this land is my land,

From California to the New York Island;

From the redwood forest to the Gulf Stream waters

This land was made for you and me.

America, America, God shed His grace on thee

And crown thy good with brotherhood

From sea to shining sea

. . . from sea to shining sea . . .

. . . From sea to shining sea . . . *Angela Jonas*

I especially like the words to *America, the Beautiful* because of the imagery. There are many different landscapes that we see in our country. We sing these two songs in our family quite often. I think it's fitting that these two songs are featured on this album as a single track. One song seems to move so naturally into the other. I had only recently noticed the cleverness of the arrangement. The first song describes the land, and the second song tells us that this great land belongs to us.

903 This Is My Country

This is my country, land of my birth
This is my country, grandest on Earth
      I pledge thee my allegiance; America, the bold
      This is my country, to have and to hold

This is my country, land of my choice
This is my country, hear my proud voice
      I pledge thee my allegiance; America, the bold
      This is my country, to have and to hold

      (. . . repeat . . .)

This is my country, land of my birth
This is my country, grandest on Earth
      I pledge thee my allegiance; America, the bold
      This is my country, to have and to hold

This is my country, land of my choice
This is my country, hear my proud voice
      I pledge thee my allegiance; America, the bold
      This is my country, to have and to hold

...my country...   *Angela Jonas*

I've had the opportunity to see quite a bit of the world. I spent two years living in east Asia as a little girl. Though it was almost 35 years years ago, my memories are still sharp. I loved the people, the scenery, the food, and the culture. I've been to Europe a number of times on vacation and enjoyed every trip. I hope to do more traveling as the opportunities arise. But of all the places on earth, I prefer to call the United States of America my home. It is "the grandest on earth; the land of my choice."

Patriotic and Community Service Memorial
Mohave High School, Bullhead City, Arizona

904 How Great Thou Art

O Lord, my God, when I in awesome wonder
Consider all the *worlds Thy hands have made
I see the stars, I hear the *rolling thunder
Thy power throughout the universe displayed

CHORUS
Then sings my soul, my Saviour God to Thee
How great Thou art, how great Thou art
Then sings my soul, my Saviour God to Thee
How great Thou art,how great Thou art

When through the woods and forest glades I wander
And hear the birds sing sweetly in the trees
When I look down from lofty mountain grandeur
And hear the brook and feel the gentle breeze
CHORUS

And when I think, that God, His Son not sparing
Sent Him to die, I scarce can take it in
That on the Cross, my burden gladly bearing
He bled and died to take away my sin
CHORUS

When Christ shall come with shout of acclamation
And take me home, what joy shall fill my heart!

Then I shall bow in humble adoration

And there proclaim, my God, how great Thou art!

CHORUS

* Author's original words are "works" and "mighty"

. . . Then sings my soul . . . *Angela Jonas*
This is another favorite of mine. Mr S. K. Hine was the writer of the English words and the arrangement was of a Swedish folk melody. I doubt that there is a person alive in the western world who doesn't recognize this beloved and familiar song. Singing this song with the help of my family was a special treat for me. I liked the country-western traditional style that we used. It brought back happy memories of family gatherings, at which old-time Christian sing-alongs always played a starring role. I hope you enjoy listening to it as much as I enjoyed singing it.

. . . awesome wonder . . .

905 Amazing Grace
Traditional

Amazing grace, how sweet the sound, that saved a wretch like me
I once was lost, but now am found; was blind, but now I see

'Twas grace that taught my heart to fear, and grace my fear relieved
How precious did that grace appear, the hour I first believed

Thru many dangers, toils and snares I have already come
'Tis grace that brought me safe thus far, and grace will lead me home

When we've been there ten-thousand years, bright shining
     as the sun
We've no less days to sing God's praise, than when we've first begun

     Amazing grace, oh, how sweet the sound, that saved a
         wretch like me
     I once was lost, oh, but now am found; was blind, but
         now I see

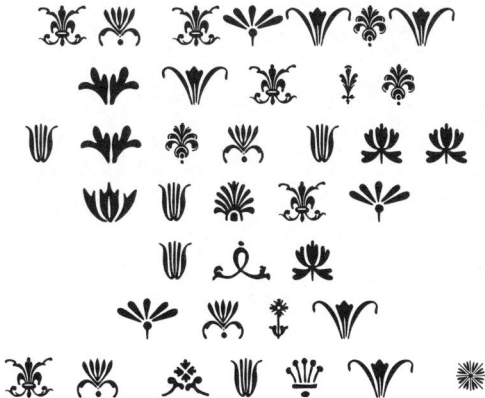

. . . how sweet the sound . . .　　　　　　　　*Angela Jonas*

I wanted to do something a little different with this song. We were all in the studio experimenting with different styles and keys, and finally ended up doing this song *a capella*, which means "without the aid of mechanical musical accompaniment." A singer friend of mine once did this song for a memorial service—a capella and as a solo. It was brilliant, and I surely have her to thank for the idea. The lyrics say it all. God's all-powerful grace saves.

Possible conclusion　　　　　　　　　　　*Dick Jonas*

One day God was sitting around in His Heaven, chin in hand, reflective crease in His brow, thinking. Turning to the attending angels and His two compadres, He said, "I believe I'll create Man."

"Create *what?*" they asked, respectfully, of course.

"Man," He reasserted.

"Great. When do we start?" asked a flag rank angel, meaning, "*how* do we start?"

Gabriel leaned over, elbowing Michael in the ribs. "What is Man?" he asked in a cosmic whisper, "and why does it begin with a capital letter?"

"Well *I* don't know," Gabriel answered, "but I think I'll stick around for awhile."

I've often wondered what He wanted with Man. He couldn't have been lonely, what with his neat little family of Jesus Christ and the Holy Spirit, plus a billion or so angels to look after. Then one day I fell in what I interpreted to be LOVE and I concluded pretty soon that this was what it was all about. LOVE is a magic, ethereal potion which overflows profusely from the heart of God. Somehow or other, it makes Him feel so much better if this unusual stuff concentrates like a laser beam and finds reception in a neat place like the human soul, than it does if all that power just rushes out to the far reaches of the Universe and dissipates into one photon per cubic mile.

I figured then that LOVE must be something like electricity — potent, explainable, quantifiable. Wrong answer. Cathodes couldn't care less if there is an anode across the way nor what happens to the electrons after launch.

So, I think that LOVE must be very special — unique, one-of-a-kind, originating solely with God. I might even venture to say that it is the prime motive force of the Universe. Perhaps LOVE is the single, unifying, ultimate TRUTH.

(ref Eccl 72111801)

906　Danny Boy

F. E. Weatherly

Oh, Danny Boy, the pipes, the pipes are calling
From glen to glen, and down the mountain side
The summer's gone and all the roses falling
It's you, it's you must go, and I must bide

But come ye back when summer's in the meadow
Or when the valley's hushed and white with snow
It's I'll be here in sunshine or in shadow
Oh, Danny Boy, oh, Danny Boy, I love you so!

But when ye come, and all the flowers are dying
If I am dead, as dead I well may be
Ye'll come and find the place where I am lying
And kneel and say an Ave there for me

And I shall hear, as soft you tread above me
And all my grave will warmer, sweeter be
For you will bend and tell me that you love me
And I shall sleep in peace until you come to me

Oh, Danny Boy, the pipes, the pipes are calling
From glen to glen, and down the mountain side
The summer's gone and all the roses falling
It's you, it's you must go, and I must bide

But come ye back when summer's in the meadow

Or when the valley's hushed and white with snow

It's I'll be here in sunshine or in shadow

Oh, Danny Boy, oh, Danny Boy, I love you so!

...such a pretty song...   *Angela Jonas*
When Dad asked me to sing *Danny Boy* for the album, I was glad for the chance to sing this classic folk favorite. The opera group I sang with always featured it at our spring concert that we did every March. Unfortunately, the person who got to sing it was almost never me. That honor generally went to the most able tenor of the group — who always did such a lovely job, by the way. It was only fair since this song is sung from a man's point of view — father to son. It's such a pretty song; simple in melodic structure with tender lyrics.

The Piper

907 Marine Hymn

Author unknown.

From the halls of Montezuma to the shores of Tripoli
We will fight our country's battles in the air, on land and sea
First to fight for right and freedom and to keep our honor clean
We are proud to claim the title of United States Marines

Our flag's unfurled to every breeze from dawn to setting sun
We have fought in every clime and place where we could take a gun
In the snows of far off northern lands and in sunny tropic scenes
You will find us always on the job — the United States Marines

Here's health to you and to our Corps which we are proud to serve
In many a strife we've fought for life and never lost our nerve
If the Army and the Navy ever looks on Heaven's scenes
They will find the streets are guarded by United States Marines

From the halls of Montezuma to the shores of Tripoli
We will fight our country's battles in the air, on land and sea
If the Army and the Navy ever looks on Heaven's scenes
They will find the streets are guarded by United States Marines

. . . proud to claim the title . . .   *Dick Jonas*

And they are. "Once a Marine, always a Marine." I think most of us are kin to a Marine, one way or another. I have this gig routine I do sometimes where I sing the service songs, usually beginning with "They Took The Blue From the Sky," for obvious reasons. When the Marine Hymn comes on, the Jarheads in the audience stop talking; they pay attention. Sometimes they stand. They *always* let me know they *are* a Marine, even if they only served one hitch.

The word "Marine" signifies harm's way. There are other terms which do that, too — infantryman, tanker, submariner — and, of course, fighter pilot. I'm glad I'm doing this in print; I expect the foregoing gauntlet could lead to a long and heated discussion.

But, y'know, there's just something about a Marine . . .

From: Jonas GySgt Timothy B
To: "Uncle Dick "
Subject: Gun Plumbers
Date: Mon, 16 Feb 2004 01:54:12 -0500

Dear Uncle Dick,

Just a quick update. We are at anchor in Cartegena
Spain; its about 00:56 in the morning.

The fellows are returning from liberty. Lance Corporal
Stinger is preparing for his Meritorious Corporal Board, to be held
on the 19th of this month. We have been at anchor since zero
eight yesterday morning — a much deserved Mediterranean port
call. Only one Marine from the ordnance shop has gotten into
trouble — because of his liberty buddy; so his luck goes. He
should have been hanging out with gun plumbers instead of operations Marines.

All the maintenance is done, except for aircraft zero six,
as she still has 500 rounds in her gun to preclude any corrosion
control on the 20mm gun system. We will get her after we pull
back out to sea. Italy was a lot of fun; Spain is fun; too. Lots of
booze to be drunk, and good chow to be had by all gun plumbers
who are not assigned to duty section. If Lance Corporal Stinger
and Lance Corporal Edwards survive the Meritorious Corporal
Board, then we may possibly have two sergeants for the next
cruise, which will commence during the month of January, 2006.

Another cruise, twenty seven more United States Marines
Aviation Ordnancemen aboard the USS Enterprise, in charge of
eleven F/A-18 Alpha Plus aircraft, to sail in support of the foreign
policy of the United States of America. Average age will be twenty
years. Each Marine will be responsible for a thirty-eight million
dollar aircraft.

They will not be afforded any "enlistment bonus," only
the promise of six months at sea. Probably will lose their girl-
friend to "old Jody boy" back home. Probably will lose any contact
with the world as they know it.

They will return to a world full of new songs, new MTV
videos. Maybe they will be close to sergeant stripes, assignment
to Parris Island as a Drill Instructor, maybe assignment to "C"
school, as an Instructor for the F/A-18 Aircraft Weapons System.

Babies will be conceived, and born. Marriages will begin,
and end; but the cycle will begin again,inevitably.

The squadron will stand down, then stand up again: workups, carrier qualifications, Fallon deployments, maintenance and inspections prior to the next cruise, when it will start all over again. Another six month deployment; new Marines will check into the squadron. They will need to be trained; the aircraft will need to be fixed for yet another carrier deployment; so much to do, and so little time to prepare. So many requirements to be met . . . And the clock continues to count . . .

We will work toward the new deployment schedule, we will watch CNN, and we will wonder when enough soldiers have died. Will there be an end? How many is enough? Can we just go over there and drop enough bombs and kill all the right bad guys to stop all the killing?

Lord knows we are always ready. Are the brass and the politicians really thinking about an end to all this bullshit?

Will there be a night when we turn to CNN and hear that there will not be anymore American soldiers dying in Iraq? That we are done with our mission? That Marine aircraft have dropped enough bombs in the right places to end all the fighting? That no one else will die?

We are out here; we are ready; we are waiting for the word. We are very good at fixing jets so they can drop bombs and shoot missiles. We are very motivated; we want to kill those individuals who are killing all our soldiers. Lord knows we have enough bombs on this ship to end any hope of resistance; we just need to know where to drop the bombs.

Maybe the chain of command will let us know. Tomorrow sounds good to all of us here in Marine Fighter Attack Squadron 312 Ordnance Shop.

Semper Fi

Tim

908   Ain't Gonna Rain No More

CHORUS
Ain't gonna rain no more, no more; it ain't gonna rain no more
Monsoon's gone, it's dry as a bone; It ain't gonna
rain no more

Well, I left my home on the Great Divide bound for California
Cash ran short, I had to abort; wound up in Arizona
CHORUS

Here I sit in the blistering heat, temperature's 120
Across from Nevada on the Lower Colorado, "Welcome to
Bullhead City!!"
CHORUS

I moved down by the river in a cardboard box, most unlucky creature
You can't live free in BHC, I took a job as a high school teacher
CHORUS

Well, I learnt real quick to do this right, a man cannot be lazy
The teenage brain is a little insane, and they'll just drive you crazy!
CHORUS

When the kids get mean and my attitude sucks, I take off
to bug smash
But you can't go fly when the heat's this high, ain't no help
at the air patch
CHORUS

When I show up at the Pearly Gates I'll tell St Pete take pity

Lemme in for a spell, I've lived in Hell; I'm from Bullhead City!

CHORUS (twice)

... Welcome to Bullhead City ...   *Dick Jonas*

Mary and I lived in Bullhead for six months, then we moved eight miles south to Fort Mojave. The weather didn't change much from one place to the other. It was hotter than the outskirts of Hell in the summer time, but other than that, we loved it. Life is laid back in Bullhead.

In the summer of 2003, the year before we moved away, I was on my way home from school one day, and I saw 126° on the car thermometer. If you're reading this in one of those progressive countries which uses the metric system, that's 52° Celsius. Frequently, BHC has the nation's high temperature in the summer.

I taught aviation to my cadets in the JROTC program. They got orientation flights in a Cessna 172. I made sure the flying happened in November through March; otherwise, the density altitudes would make the exercise somewhat problematic.

It didn't rain much. The climatology called for four inches a year, but during the decade we were there, the southwestern United States was in the grip of a long term drought. I don't think we got half that. The good news is, BHC sits exactly on the banks of the lower Colorado River.

I never thought I wanted to live in Bullhead. But, I'm glad we did. Teaching Air Force Junior ROTC was probably the most worthwhile thing I've ever done in the blue suit.

909   Futures

When I get through with this man's war and out of this man's army
The kind of life I'm looking for is one that cannot harm me
No, not for me the speedy plane I used to pot the Hun with
A second-handed little Ford will do to have my fun with

This thing of dodging through the skies has made me
              tense and nervous
I'll make my tours in Pullman seats when I am through the service
And bump to work in trolley cars like other city dwellers
And thank my stars I'm not behind the blast of air propellers

              That's me when I don't have to fly with army aviators
              The only time I'll ever climb will be in elevators

When I am through with this man's war and out of this man's army
I'll be a person who'll abhor whatever might alarm me
For after months of split-tail stunts and wild and reckless chances
It's me to play things safe and sane in placid circumstances

I'll take my risks in auction bridge and penny-ante poker
Where there's no German Fokker bus to be the little joker
Let others gamble in the games of danger and endurance
My family will be old and gray when they get my insurance

I'll never take the jobs that make a fellow's frame grow thinner
I plan to plod, acquire a pod, and nod each night at dinner

My bus? It's that one over there. Some traveler, that baby
And when I'm through, well, yes, sometimes I'll
    think about her, maybe
And dream of shoutin' "Contact, boys!" and of her motor roaring
And taxiing along the field, lifting, zooming, soaring

Just now, what looks the best to me is peace and rest and quiet
I'm planning for the simple life and hoping when I try it
That I won't find this Spad of mine still has the lure to charm me
And make me dream of this man's war and long for this man's army

    Say, but she's trim and swift and slim as through the
        clouds I weave her
    And I'll admit that when I quit I sure will hate to leave her!

SPAD XVI
USAF Museum

Spad 16

. . . Say, but she's trim and swift and slim . . .

910   GIB Named Richard

Now let me tell you the story of a GIB named Richard
And the way that he did fail
He planned out the target, grabbed his trusty old hammer
Went to fly a Commando Nail
> Did he ever return? Yes, he surely returned
> With his scope film in his hand
> When the DCO saw his documentation
> He said, "I wanta see that man!"

Richard's OAP was a place called Dong Hoi
And the sun was at his back
He stuck his head in the scope, then he ran out the cursors
Thinking, "This time I've got a shack!"
> Did he ever return? Yes, he surely returned
> Thinking he'd performed in style
> Unfortunately, when the film was developed
> He had missed by seven miles

Well, Colonel Meroney picked himself off the ceiling
Screaming loudly, "Fuck - shit - hate!
Get me Compton and Cox and get 'em here in a hurry
To consider Richard's fate!"
> Did they ever return? Did they _ever_ return!
> They were there post-haste, you bet!
> The colonel said, "Take Dick off the schedule
> He's the worst that I've seen yet!"

Now all day long Richard sits around the squadron
Crying, "Who will fly with me?
All I need is only ten more counters
Until Frisco Bay I see . . ."

      Did he ever come back? Yes, he made a comeback
      They made Dick one special good deal
      Said, "You'll be back on status, just put five 750's
      Down the smokestack of Ho's steel mills!"

Very early next morning, then, we found poor Richard
With his scope film in his hand
He was all set to go bomb the mills at Thai Nguyen
Said, "I'll show 'em I'm a radar man!"

      Will he ever return? Will he ever return?
      Will he learn to radar bomb?
      If he ever comes back, next it's Huu Hung Ferry
      Then we'll send poor Richard home

F-4 Phantom II
Huu Hung Ferry, here we come!

9 1 1   Bless 'Em All

Bless 'em all, bless 'em all

The long and the short and the tall

Bless all the sergeants and WO-1s

Bless all the corporals and their blooming sons

We're saying goodbye to them all

The long and the short and the tall

You'll get no promotion this side of the ocean

Cheer up, my lads, bless 'em all

Bless 'em all, bless 'em all

The long and the short and the tall

Bless old man Lockheed for building this jet

I know a guy who is cursing him yet

He tried to go over the wall

With his tiptanks, tailpipe and all

The needles did cross and the wings they came off

Cheer up, my lads, bless 'em all

Bless 'em all, bless 'em all

The needle, the airspeed, the ball

Bless those instructors who taught me to fly

Sent me to solo and left me to die

If ever your blow-jet should stall

You're in for one hell of a fall

No lilies, no violets for dead fighter pilots

Cheer up, my lads, bless 'em all

Bless 'em all, bless 'em all

The long and the short and the tall

Bless all the sergeants and their bloody sons

Bless all the corporals, the fat-headed ones

9-23

I'm saying goodbye to them all

The long and the short and the tall

To you and the others, just shove it up, brothers!

I'm going back home in the fall

. . . bless 'em all . . . bless 'em all . . . bless 'em all . . .

. . . The needle, the airspeed, the ball . . .   *Dick Jonas*

Listen to Jimmy Buffet sing his own special brand of sea-chanties. The music he writes and sings is about him — about sailing boats, the islands, the water.

Makes me think about the kind of songs I write and sing, about flying airplanes. I guess I was luckier than most aviators, because the airplanes I flew had a lot more to do, up there in the sky, than people normally think about. For most folks an airplane is for getting from point A to point B without scaring the shit out of you.

Me and my compadres — we took those airplanes up there in the sky to fight with people, drop bombs, blow things up, tear stuff up. You do a helluva lot more with a fighter than you do up in the sky with most other airplanes.

I guess this is "folk" music. It's what the "folks" sing. If the "folks" happen to be bum sailors down in the Carribbean, they sound a lot like Buffet. If they happen to be bum fighter pilots, they sing about flying and fighting.

Cowboys. People are still writing cowboy songs. Decades, generations, after the sho-nuff cowboy branded his last heifer.

Truck driving songs. Remember when the country music field was mostly truck driving songs? Not any more. It worries me a little bit.

Most of the songs I wrote were about the Vietnam War. I've written a bunch more since then about flying airplanes that don't have anything to do with Vietnam.

Truck driving songs came and went. The Vietnam genre never came. That means it ain't "went" yet. And those of us who had our day in the sun in that generation are still laying around in the weeds, nursing our arthritis, wheel chairs and oxygen bottles, hoping someday somebody will pay attention to what we did in Vietnam.

You know, listen to our songs, and say "shit-hot" and "rah-rah" and clap their hands a lot. And spend their money on our music, like they do on the cowboys, and the truck drivers, and Buffet.

(ref Eccl 93080402)

9 1 2   Teak Lead

Air Force traditional. Via Bill Getz in *The Wild Blue Yonder.* Arrangement
©2002 Dick Jonas. All rights reserved.

To the valley he said he was flying
And he never saw the medal that he earned
Many jocks have flown into the valley
And a number have never returned

So, I listened as he briefed on the mission
Tonight at the bar Teak Flight will sing
For we're going to the Red River Valley
And today you are flying my wing

Oh, the flak is so thick in the valley
That the MiGs and the missiles we don't need
So fly high and down-sun in the valley
And guard well the ass of Teak Lead

Now, if things turn to shit in the valley
And the brief that I gave you don't heed
They'll be waiting at the Hanoi Hilton
And it's fish heads and rice for Teak Lead

We refueled on the way to the valley
In the States it had always been fun
But, with thunder and lightning all around us
'Twas the last AAR for Teak One

We came to a bridge in the valley
There it lay in the late morning sun
And the first to roll in on the target
Was my leader, Old Teak Number One

He flew through the flak toward the target
In a dive with his pipper drew a bead
But he never pulled off of the bomb run
Farewell to another Teak Lead

So come and sit by my side at the briefing
We will sit there and tickle the beads
For we're going to the Red River Valley
And my call sign today is Teak Lead
    . . . My call sign today is Teak Lead . . .

Luck   *Irv LeVine*

They say there's good luck and bad luck. But, what do you do when yours seems all bad? What is bad luck, anyway; and how does it attach itself to you? A black cat crossing your path? How about 'never-light-three-on-a-match?

What wards it off? Throwing salt over your left shoulder? Prayer? Being good? And, does it always come in threes?

To paraphrase Henny Youngman, "Take Teak Lead. Please!"

There's no rhyme, reason, circumstance or level of superstition that will guarantee a bad outcome . . . or is there? What wards off hot, molten, steel fragments coming at you from an exploding triple-A shell, courtesy of an inspired, angry gunner thousands of feet below you?

Well; the new Teak Lead will soon find out. He's leading the 16 ship gaggle to Hanoi this morning and it's almost briefing time.

Damn! Where's Roscoe when you need him?

913 TV Commercials

Television's making me a nervous wreck the way they advertise
Just about the time the climax comes there's a pause
commercial-wise

CHORUS
TV commercials are driving me nuts I'm a borderline
mental case
The next time somebody says buy something
I'm gonna quit the human race

The Jolly Green Giant hollers "Ho, ho, ho!" in my dreams at night
Mr Clean's shaving with a coo-coo brand and he'd rather switch
than fight

Last night Marshall Dillon drew his gun on the meanest
man alive
Just about the time two shots were fired
Come a word from VO-5

The Man from Uncle was in a fix, he was being sent to Mars
Just when the rocket ship blasted off it was time for trading cars

38% fewer cavities, soap suds ten feet tall
If I see any more headache pills
I'm gonna climb a wall

CHORUS

. . . driving me nuts . . .   *Dick Jonas*

I wrote this silly thing while I was in college, but I didn't record it until 2002, so it never got any air play. I don't know that it has since '02, either. I was living in Valdosta, Georgia and still in possession of my first lil 'ole black and white TV. Timing is everything, they say, and the programmers are masters at shutting down the action at just the right point for a commercial to make sure you're gonna be back when it's over.

The Classics   *Dick Jonas*

Speaking of programming, I can't believe that all this noise masquerading as music on the radio these days is liked by people!

I know what's going on. The programmer at the radio station, or the DJ, or whoever picks out the damn music and decides what gets played, thinks, "Well, I don't like this one, but it's popular and everbody else does." So he plays it.

Turns out that NObody likes the thing. Nobody. So a lot of shit gets played that nobody likes. It's perceived peer pressure, just like happens with teenagers in school. It's "in," and nobody has the guts to take a stand on quality.

I think that's why oldies stations are so popular. Those songs have stood the test of time. Those songs are what people liked best of all the crap that came over the airwaves. What if the oldies stations played the next forty, just beneath the top 100? They'd die before sundown.

The proof of quality is attested by the young people today who really like the good stuff from generations ago.

There's something indescribably magic about the quality of truly good music which reaches straight into the viscera of humans, no matter their generation, and says, "Hey! We meet again. Remember me? This is quality. This is goodness. This is beauty. This is real music."

And their souls resonate with the natural, unalterable truth. That's why kids who were not even a twinkle in anybody's eye when Chuck Berry belted out "Johnny Be Good" the first time think he's the neatest thing since Seven-Up.

I'll betcha the bastards never wise up. The music programmers, I mean. For the rest of our natural lives, for as long as there's radio, there'll be a whole shit-load of trash, half or better of whatever's gonna be played, that ain't worth a damn.

They'll do it. "Well; I don't like it, but 'everybody' else does, and I gotta be 'cool,' so I better play this crap . . . "

(ref Eccl 93080404)

9-28

914 Drugstore Cowboy

I'm just a drugstore cowboy, give me a water gun for a toy
Show me where to look for a western comic book
I'm just a drugstore cowboy

>Give me a rocky horse to ride
>Give me a six-gun by my side
>Give me a hat three feet wide
>Let me sit and watch "Rawhide"

I'm just a drugstore cowboy, western movies make me jump for joy
The meanest cowpoke that ever sat and watched "Gunsmoke"
Is me; I'm a drugstore cowboy

>Turn my TV set to "Wagon Train"
>I've got western movies on the brain
>Why, I'd sit and watch 'em in the rain
>Cowboy shows are my own ball and chain

My head-shrinker says I shouldn't see all them cowboy shows on TV
I tied him with a rope, then I fed him saddle soap
Like I seen 'em do on "Laramie"

>Gene Autry really makes me flip
>The way he gives Geronimo the slip
>Gene fights 'em twenty at a clip
>Where Gene's concerned, I just don't take no lip

John Wayne and Richard Boone are fine

I go to see their movies all the time

I learned to handle guns just by watching old reruns

Of cowboy shows on that TV of mine

I watch Bonanza every Sunday night

Ben and Adam, Hoss and Joe Cartwright

I've watched 'em drink but never seen 'em tight

And I ain't never seen 'em lose a fight

I'm just a drugstore cowboy,western movies make me jump for joy

Show me where to look for a western comic book

Call me a drugstore cowboy

Change   *Dick Jonas*

I LUV the American west. These cowboy shows and characters remind me of a trip I made once from Reno to Colorado Springs . . .

Spent last night at Green River State Park. Hot showers; place to shave. Fire pit; you can cook your supper. And it's right on the Green River, the muddiest, most opaque—most? Either it's opaque, or it ain't—stream I've seen since I played Operation Jayhawk with the field grade grunts on the Kansas plains.

Beautiful night; severe clear. Whipped out the ole geetar and entertained myself for awhile before the rack monster got me in a half-nelson. Or is it a half-gainer? I never can remember; that's what I get for being a musician, instead of a jock-strap.

Interstate 70, eastbound for C-Springs. Think I'll detour through Aspen, and say hello to Heinz E. Coordes.

Got to thinking: Change is the normal human condition. The only thing that doesn't change, is change itself.

Look back on your life. It's true; tastes you have now are not what you had a few years back.

However. For each of us, there is that special little cherished quirk which remains always the same.

Take me, for instance; I never got over tits, guitars and airplanes.

(ref Eccl 93082301)

10

Dick Jonas & Irv LeVine

Live At Leeuwarden

with the RNLAF 322nd Fighter Squadron

"The Pollies"

EROSONIC   Album Ten

As with any live show, you play and sing what the audience wants to hear. That's what we did at Leeuwarden. Consequently, in this chapter there will be some repetition of material found in this book's predecessor, *RBAAB: The Red-Blooded, All-American Boy.* There are, however, several new songs we've never recorded before. You will find a definite Dutch flavor here.

EROSONIC

Irv Igor Dick

Dick Woody

June 2003, and the RNLAF 322nd Fighter Squadron is celebrating it's 60th anniversary. Spitfires in the 40s, Meteors and Hunters in the 50s, Starfighters in the 60s and transition to the F-16 Viper in the 80s. Oivind Jervan ("Igor"), a Norwegian fighter pilot on exchange duty with the 322, invites Dick Jonas and Irv LeVine to come over and help celebrate. HUGE blast! Just like old times — Friday night rowdy happy hour in the O'Club, then a Saturday air show and another sing-along in the hangar that night.

Pyro Igor

DON'T TALK

NIET PRATEN
322 322
MAAR DOEN

JUST ACT

1001 Hey, Mr Taliban (AAAAAAAYO! AAAAAAYO!)

HAAAAAAAYO! HAAAAAAYO!
> Air Force come, gonna flatten your home

First, World War Two and then Korea
Air Force come gonna flatten your home
Then Vietnam and now diarrhea
Air Force come, gonna flatten your home

CHORUS

> Hey! Mr. Taliban we know where you're hiding
> Air Force come gonna flatten your home
> Hey! Mr. Taliban we know where you're hiding
> Air Force come, gonna flatten your home

The stealth fighter come, mon, you ain't gon' see it
Air Force come gonna flatten your home
Then B-52's, mon, you ain' gon' believe it
Air Force come, gonna flatten your home

A sixty foot, seventy foot, eighty foot crater
Air Force come gonna flatten your home
Uncle Sam's pissed, mon, he ain' no Quaker
Air Force come, gonna flatten your home

CHORUS

When we done you all be cryin'

Air Force come gonna flatten your home

The pilots are brothers of the New York firemen

Air Force come, gonna flatten your home

AAAAAY U.S.A., U.S.A. U.S.AAAAY-O

Air Force come, gonna flatten your home

... **AAAAAAYO!** ...   *Irv LeVine*
Inspired by the outstanding selflessness of the firemen
who died in New York City on 9-11, and our ability to bring the
war to the Taliban in their own back yard.

F-16 vs Osama

He's gonna wish he had chaff and flares . . . and afterburner.

1002 Nickel On the Grass

Air Force traditional. Arrangement ©1997 Dick Jonas. All rights reserved.

CHORUS

Hallelujah! Hallelujah!
Throw a nickel on the grass save a fighter pilot's ass
Hallelujah! Hallelujah!
Throw a nickel on the grass and you'll be safe!

I'm cruising down the Yalu, doing six-and-twenty per
I cried to my flight leader, "Oh, won't you save me, Sir!
Got two big flak holes in my wings, my engine's outta gas!
Mayday! Mayday! Mayday! Got six MiGs on my ass!"

CHORUS

I shot my traffic pattern, to me it looked alright
The airspeed read one-ninety, I really racked it tight
The airframe gave a shudder, the engine gave a wheeze
Mayday! Mayday! Mayday! Spin instructions please!

CHORUS

The crosswind blew me side ways, the left wing hit the ground
I firewalled the throttle, and I tried to go around
I yanked that Sabre in the air, a dozen feet or more
The engine quit, I almost shit, the gear came through the floor

CHORUS

Nickel, or Nipple . . . ?   *Dick Jonas*

This is one of the older fighter pilot songs — among the first I ever learned. It gets it said, it's easy to play and sing, and most everybody knows it. So, I sing it a lot; and, I get lots of help doing it. The "Royal Goddam Dutch" are no different. They pitched right in.

If you haven't been to Chapter 12 yet, there's a new twist to this thing.

F-86 Sabre

Two things: That looks like a 67 TFS patch beneath the canopy rail; and the terrain below looks a lot like Korea.

⊕ ✳ ✱ ✺

✳ ⚹ ✿ 🔥 ♖ ♈ ⚘ ❄

Reverse osmosis . . .

"Those who can, do. Those who can't, teach. Those who can't teach, write."

— And the teachers teach what is written, and the doers do what is taught, and the writers sit back and collect royalties.

This is the same process by which hotrock jet fighter pilots fly up their own tailpipes.

(ref Eccl 93020901)

1003 Son of Satan's Angels

CHORUS

I'm a Son of Satan's Angels and I fly the F-4D
All the way from the Hanoi Railroad Bridge to the DMZ
I'm one of old Hoot Gibson's boys and mean as I can be
I'm a Son of Satan's Angels and I fly the F-4D

There ain't a triple-A gunner up there that's anywhere near my class
'Cause I'm as mad as I can be and I'm in for one more pass
He hosed me down one time too much and that one is his last
I can see my CBUs tearing holes in the gunner's ass

CHORUS

Hello, Hanoi Hanna, send your MiGs to meet their doom
Light 'em up and blast 'em off, Hoot's boys will be there soon
I don't care if you are the gal with a mouth full of silver spoon
'Cause I got Sidewinders on board that'll home on an AB plume

CHORUS

Robin's Phantom   *Dick Jonas*

On page 7-22 is a picture of Robin Olds' Phantom. That bird belonged to Satan's Angels. It's in the Air Force Museum in Dayton. While I never flew with him, I've always been intrigued by the fact that we did fly some of the same air frames. I'm particularly proud to be a Son of Satan's Angels.

433rd Tac Fighter Squadron

. . . one of old Hoot Gibson's boys . . .

1004 Korean Waterfall

Author unknown. Air Force traditional. Arr ©2005 Dick Jonas. All rights reserved.

Beside a Korean waterfall on a cold and cloudy day
Beside his busted Sabre Jet the young pursuiter lay
His parachute hung from a nearby tree, he was not yet quite dead
Listen to the very last words the young pursuiter said

"I'm going to a better land where everything's all right
Where whiskey flows from telegraph poles, play poker every night
There's not a single thing to do, but sit around and sing
And all the crews are women; oh death, where is thy sting?

"Death, where is thy sting, ting-a-ling? Oh, death, where is thy sting?
The bells of Hell will ring, ting-a-ling, for you! But, not for me!

"So-o-o, ring-a-ling-a-ling-ting; blow it out your ass
Ring-a-ling-a-ling-ting; blow it out your ass
Ring-a-ling-a-ling-ting; blow it out your ass
Better days are coming, bye-and-bye!"

There's a skeeter on my peter, knock 'im off
There's a skeeter on my peter, knock 'im off
There's a skeeter on my peter, there's a skeeter on my peter
There's a skeeter on my peter, knock 'im off

There's another on your brother, knock 'im off
There's another on your brother, knock it off
There's another on your brother, there's another on your brother
There's another on your brother, knock 'im off

There's a dozen on your cousin, knock 'em off
There's a dozen on your cousin, knock 'em off
There's a dozen on your cousin, can't you hear them bastards buzzin'
There's a dozen on your cousin, knock 'em off

Skeeter   *Dick Jonas*
    This is another among the first fighter pilot songs I ever learned and sang. The part about the 'skeeter' I learned many years after the traditional song. I cannot remember where I got that part.
    I don't always sing the skeeter part; it depends on the crowd. I'm a slightly timid fighter pilot; it's more important to me to be liked and appreciated, than it is to make a spectacle of myself. If it's just me and my buds — male and/or female — I do the whole banana. Always gets a chuckle.

UPT Squadron
1966. Moody AFB GA. Class 67-C

1005 Pull the Boom From the Gashole

CHORUS

Pull that boom from the gashole, Tanker, let me go
Clear me out of the anchor track before the sun sinks low
I got a buddy on the ground up north in Route Pack Four
Pull that pipe from the gashole, Boomer, let me go

We rolled in on a bridge up north about daylight
And the guns on the ground was a-lookin' for a fight
Pulling out we got hosed pretty good with ZPU
And they shot off the starboard wing of Wolfpack Two

CHORUS

Old Wolfpack Two was on the beeper when he hit the ground
I told him, "Don't go nowhere, just hang around
I got a Jolly Green Giant coming in, in a little while
Hang loose, ole buddy, we'll bring you home in style."

CHORUS

Well, ole Sandy came in first with nape and fifty-cal
And that Super Jolly Green looked good as a round-eyed gal
Wolfpack Two spent the night down south at NKP
With a tall Sing-hi and a poo-yeng on his knee

CHORUS

10-11

. . . the gashole . . .   *Dick Jonas*

We were redeploying from Norway once. Buddied with
KCs for seven IFRs. It was clear and a million all the way. Over
Labrador, it got pretty turbulent — CAT (clear air turbulence.)
I'm in an F-16 and it's a little like going over Niagara Falls in a
barrel. The tanker, on the other hand, was getting his wings
flapped like a buzzard on take-off from a road kill. I remarked to
the tanker pilot that I didn't believe I'd ever seen a tank do acro
before. He didn't see much humor in my comment.

KC-135R & Vipers

. . . this is the way we go to war, go to war, go to war . . .

Fighter pilots and lawyers

South of Boulder Dam, southbound for Phoenix. Thinking
about the difference between fighter pilots and lawyers.

. . . (*Cynical* chuckle) . . .

. . . There ain't much . . .

Well; there is — a lot. In some ways we're quite dissimi-
lar. Fighter pilots are cocky; lawyers are arrogant.

I think the difference between cocky and arrogant may be
that cocky can laugh at itself. Arrogance, on the other hand, *will*
be taken seriously; no one may laugh at it without retribution.

For example, you ever hear lawyers tell each other lawyer
jokes?

(ref Eccl 94011402)

1006 Yodel-de-O

I went across to Switzerland
To find a girl; I was a lonely man
I found her there; gave her a kiss
We sing together; it sounds like this

CHORUS

Yodel-de-O, yodel-de-O, yodel-de-O, yodel-de-O
Yodel-de-O, yodel-de-O, yodel-de-odel-de-odel-de-odel-de-O

I married her; we settled down
In a little brown house close to town
We had some kids; oh, two or three
And now they sing with her and me

CHORUS

Her dad made cheese — the kind called Swiss
Our love gave us perfect bliss
But singing or eating that old Swiss cheese
The sounds we made came out like these

CHORUS

(. . . yodel finale . . .)

World Champeen Yodeler   *Dick Jonas*

The pic below was shot during a lull in the raucous action at the Leeuwarden O'Club, on Friday night, 13 June 2003.

Two weeks prior, we'd conducted a working rehearsal with the "Pollies" in San Diego. They were deployed to the States for an exercise.

I taught them "Wild West Show" and Irv taught them "Yodel-de-O." They were a quick study, and I got a feeling there were some impromptu rehearsals between then and the show at Leeuwarden. Anyway, by the time we did it in the club, they were ready.

You can't really appreciate a yodel until you've heard it done by a rowdy bunch of fighter jocks with a Dutch accent!

Happy Hour at the Leeuwarden O'Club
Irv, Sally, an incognito AFE jock, Woody

1007 Thanh Hoa Bridge

CHORUS

On the day Thanh Hoa Bridge saw the light
The guys from the Wolfpack went up north to fight
We did our thing like we oughter
We dropped that bridge in the water
On the day Thanh Hoa Bridge saw the light

There's a lot of good planes in the mud around Thanh Hoa Bridge
And a lot of parachutes laying out on Thanh Hoa Ridge
And the guys that took 'em North can't go nowhere
All because of the guns on the ground around Thanh Hoa Bridge

CHORUS

So we put our heads together one night around a tall Sing-hi
Trying to figure out a way to kill a bridge that didn't really wanta die
We talked it up to the boys with the bombs with the brains
And they allowed to kill the Thanh Hoa Bridge wouldn't take no strain

CHORUS

GBU-31/32 Joint Direct Attack Munition (JDAM)
National Museum of the USAF

JDAM

This one didn't kill Thanh Hoa Bridge; it's grandpappy did.

Fractured Fractions   *Dick Jonas*

Missions to places like the Thanh Hoa bridge could leave a guy needing a drink pretty badly. That got me to thinking . . . One Kilocalorie = 3087.3 foot-pounds of energy. So if I move my 150-pound weight a distance of 20.6 feet, I will use up one kilocalorie. If I drink 12 ounces of beer containing 150 Kcal, I need to move my 150-pound bod a distance of 3090 feet; that's six-tenths of a mile. Now, my custom is to run/walk three miles a day, three days a week. That's just under one six-pack per day for each day that I run. In actuality, I drink on the average, two six-packs a week. It takes two days of running to cancel those two out. Then the third day of running is what makes my body lean, mean, slim, trim and pretty.

And oh-by-the-way, don't forget the aerobic benefits of running which accrue to my heart, respiratory system and blood pressure; not to mention the smug satisfaction I get out of telling my friends, "Yeh. I run three miles a day." (. . . And don't forget to tack on a Barney Fife sniff at the end of that comment . . .)

This stuff is neat! One beer will melt four pounds of ice or boil a half-gallon of water.

Footnote: My weight, drinking habits, and exercise patterns have changed significantly since I wrote this in 1985.

(ref Eccl 85100402)

1008 Give Me Operations

Author unknown. Air Force traditional. Arr ©2003 Dick Jonas and Irv LeVine.

CHORUS

Give me operations, way out on some lonely atoll
For I am too young to die, I just want to grow old

Don't give me a P-38, the props they counter-rotate
She's smattered from Burma to Britain
Don't give me a P-38

CHORUS

Don't give me an 86D, with rockets, radar, and AB
It's fast, I don't care, it blows up in mid-air
Don't give me an 86D

CHORUS

Don't give me a one double-oh, to fight against friendly or foe
That old Sabre dance made me crap in my pants
Don't give me a one double-oh

CHORUS

Don't give me a B-52, it carries one hell of a crew
Yeah, there's lotsa guys, but they're all SACemcized
Don't give me B-52

CHORUS

Just give me a sweet F-16, you've seen her, you know what I mean
She's very high tech, and she's better than sex
Just give me an F-sweet-sixteen

CHORUS

Don't give me an F-105, 'cause I like being alive
She's great for attack, she soaks up mach-mach flak
Dont' give me an F-105

CHORUS

Operations *Dick Jonas*
Flying operations, that is — so as not to confuse the flight surgeons.
This song is a lot like "Aye - Yi - Yi - Yi." If we were to sing *all* the verses, to include all the airplanes, it would take about a week, I think. If you want more, see *RBAAB: The Red-Blooded, All-American Boy*, page 5-11and the two pages following.
Thus far, I"ve not heard verses for the A-10, the F-22, the F-35, most of the bombers, and none of the airlifters and trainers. So, there's fertile ground still to be cultivated here.

✿ ✿ ✿ ❦ ✿ ✿
✿ ✿ ✿ ✿ ✿

Never mind me. I am a wingman. I am expendable.
(ref Eccl 92091001)
"Major deer crossing area ahead."
What if I see a deer with stripes? Could be a zebra. Ha.
(ref Eccl 92092101)

God did a much better job with the brain than He did with the body. I'll bet He's out there working on that right now.
(ref Eccl 25011502)

1009 Superman

All day, all night, Mary Ann; all day, all night, Mary Ann
All day, all night, Mary Ann
Who in the hell do you think I am? Superman?

Man of steel   *Dick Jonas*
    Though he was the reddest-blooded, all-American boy
Krypton had to offer, Superman routinely defied Nature's laws.

Weight, Mass, and Inertia. And the Metric System.

    Speaking of Nature's laws, an ABC News lackey has
just informed me that the astronauts aboard Endeavour — on its
maiden voyage by the way — have finally gotten their hands on
that errant four-and-a-half ton satellite. As happens too often,
the newsman is misinformed; the satellite weighs nothing. The
concept of weight in space is meaningless. "Weight" has meaning
only in the presence of gravity. He would more correctly refer to
the big satellite as "massive." An object which weighs four-and-a-
half tons (9,000 pounds) at the surface of the Earth has a mass
of 281.5 slugs. Quaint concept, slugs. It is a measure of mass
and corresponds to kilograms in the metric system, as pounds
weight corresponds to newtons. The 9,000 pound satellite weighs
39,600 newtons.

We Americans simply must join the rest of the world in
how we measure things. Nobody understands what we are talking about.

Anyway. Is the satellite subject to gravity? Most definitely. If it were not, it would have floated out to Betelgeuse long
ago. It is the gravitational attraction of the Earth which keeps
the thing in orbit — as it does Endeavour, TIROS the weather
satellite, GPS Navstar, and G1 which brings me The Discovery
Channel.

How much gravity does that take? Not much. Certainly
not as much as it does to keep my feet firmly planted on the floor
of my office.

The correct term is "microgravity." "Micro." That's one-
millionth. (A *micro*scope would be one-millionth of a scope . . . ;)

Actually, a microscope enables one to visually observe objects which are the tiniest of the tiny. In any event, the microgravity acting upon Endeavour and its hitchhiker is not nearly enough to warrant the reference to four-and-a-half tons.

It's time for the media to graduate from the eighth grade and stop telling the world how much things *weigh* in space. They need to tell us how *massive* things are. In space, mass and its big brother, inertia, are the operative concepts. So long as the media, with its (mis)interpretation of science refuses to acknowledge concepts codified hundreds of years ago by such luminaries as Newton and Kepler, I fear that humanity will forever have its feet mired in the clay. We may never reach the stars.

(ref Eccl 92051301)

Mike Haywood says time is what keeps everything from happening all at once.

(ref Eccl 92030202)

Shovel Work In Space

Putting the arm on a satellite.

1010 My Father Was a Fireman

Oh, for the life of a fireman, to drive a fire engine red. To say to a team of white horses, "Go ahead! Go ahead! Give me head!"

My father was a fireman; he puts out fires
My brother was a fireman; he puts out fires
My sister, Sal, was a fireman's gal; she puts out, too

Fireman, hey . . . ?   *Dick Jonas*

Some fighter pilot songs do not tell a story, do not regale the world with the attitudes and exploits of the cocky sky warrior — in point of fact, are not war songs at all. They're just rowdy and cute and reflect the little boy mentality typical of most young warriors of ground, sea, and sky.

My Father Was a Fireman is a prime example of the sub genre.

If you look around — in this book, in its predecessor, in the myriad organizational song books floating around out there, you will surely find others similar.

"A"Flight

13th Fighter Squadron, Udorn RTAFB Thailand

Reno Routine

Guys who fly racing and stunt planes at Reno every fall are a different breed of cat — like combat flyers.

If a hot rock racing plane pilot seems so calm, cool, collected, and nonchalant, it's because he's formed a habit pattern of making his flying routine. That's exactly how you want dangerous flying — or dangerous anything — to be.

Routine . . . You do what you're supposed to do when you're supposed to do it and everything happens like it's supposed to happen. It's kinda like putting your pants on in the morning when you get up. Or shaving.

It's not that racing plane pilots are smug and egotistical, it's that they've developed a frame of reference, an attitude, that makes them safe and hopefully makes them win.

(ref Eccl 92092106)

1011 Wild West Show

Author unknown. Air Force traditional. Arrangement ©2003 Dick Jonas. All rights reserved.

CHORUS
We're off to see the wild west show, the elephants and the kangaroo
No matter what the weather, as long as we're together
We're off to see the wild west show

In this corner, ladies and gentlemen, we have the oo-ah bird
Fantastic! Incredible! No shit! Tell us about the mother-fucker!
The oo-ah bird has legs that are two feet long and a scrotum which is three feet long. When he comes in for a landing, he cries, "OO! AH! OO! AH!"

CHORUS

In this corner, ladies and gentlemen, we have the Fukawi tribe
Fantastic! Incredible! No shit! Tell us about the mother-fucker!
The Fukawi are a tribe of people who are three feet tall and live in a savanna where the grass is six feet tall. All day long they wander around crying, "Where the Fukawi!? Where the Fukawi!?"

CHORUS

In this corner, ladies and gentlemen, we have the Kee-Kee bird
Fantastic! Incredible! No shit! Tell us about the mother-fucker!
The Kee-Kee bird has the highest thrust and the lowest wing loading of any flying machine known to man.

He flies in ever-decreasing concentric circles until he flies up his own asshole; and you can hear him say, "Kee-kee-kee-rist, it's dark in here!"

CHORUS

In this corner, ladies and gentlemen, we have the Kee-Kee bird, Mod One.

"Fantastic! Incredible! No shit! Tell us about the mother-fucker!"

The Kee-Kee bird, Mod One, is fond of Stuka-like dive bomb passes. He points his nose STRAIGHT down, winds it up to a Mach-and-a-half, and holds it 'til he can stand it no longer. On pullout, you'll hear him cry, "Kee-Kee-Kee-rist, that was close!"

CHORUS

In this corner, ladies and gentlemen, we have Lulu, the tatooed lady.

"Fantastic! Incredible! No shit! Tell us about the mother-fucker!"

Lulu, the tatooed lady, has a big "W" tattoed on one cheek. On the other she has another big "W." When she stands up on her feet it says "WoW!" When she stands on her head, it says "MoM!" And when she does cartwheels, it says, "WoW, MoM! WoW, Mom!"

CHORUS

. . . the elephants and the kangaroo . . . ?   *Irv LeVine*

Dick introduced me to this one. It's his fault. (And me with a picture of my sainted mother in my back pocket.) Still, this audience participation song, sung late at almost any gig, will bring an audience to it's feet in howling anticipation. They're only words and if they give some release from the tremendous mental strain from the hours of boredom, stress and fear that ride in every cockpit on a possible mission of no return I'M FOR IT. Take it away Dick . . . I've got the second verse . . .

10-24

1012 Sally In the Alley

Sally in the alley sifting cinders

Lifted up her leg and farted like a man

Wind from her bloomers broke six winders

Cheeks of her ass went Bam! Bam! Bam!

...*flying fighters* ...   *Dick Jonas*

Highway 93, enroute to Vegas. About ten miles north of Wickieup. Near where Chris and I saw the space shuttle that time . . .

How come fighter pilots don't seem to have any corporate memory? Not too long ago, I went out and partied with some of the Strike Eagle troops at Luke. They were nice enough to have some of my tapes playing on their cosmic stereo. The older guys thought that was really shit-hot, to play ole Dick Jonas's songs, and have him out there drinking beer and eating chicken wings with 'em.

The other guys, however — the slick-wings — didn't seem to respond as enthusiastically as I (chuckle) could have wished. At first, I mean; it got better later on. We got the geetar out and started picking and singing dirty fighter pilot songs. It began to look a lot like old times.

But I don't think the young guys really relate very much to all those cosmic war-fighting songs I wrote about Vietnam. I don't think it's necessarily because Vietnam was kind of a tawdry little thing, or that this younger generation has "gone to the dogs," or sump'n like that. I remember when I was a rock-'em sock-'em thirty-year-old captain doing some of the same things those guys are doing right now, there just wasn't room in my life and in my thoughts for anything but me. And my compadres. And the machine we were flying. And the job we were doing on a daily, routine basis.

What happened in the past doesn't have that large of an impact on the new beans. All they care about is what happens yesterday, today and tomorrow: And I do mean that 72-hour snapshot which constitutes the fighter pilot's great eternal now.

Ten years ago is non-existent; ten years from now they're gonna be in a staff job and wondering how they could ever have been so stupid as to trade in a supersonic cockpit for a desk — or retired, or flying for the airlines, a lot of 'em. Their lives are totally full of what's happening today.

So I guess I shouldn't be too surprised if I walk into a fighter jock bar where some of my old fart friends who are still on active duty have my music playing, and the slick-wings are not paying attention.

. . . A minute-and-a-half down the road; let's continue that thought a little bit . . .

I expect the business of flying fighters is not the only place where this phenomenon occurs. All morning, ever since I launched from Phoenix for Vegas, I've had this comparison running through my mind, between fighter pilots and stock brokers. I suspect the difference between the two is not a great deal. There is a little bit, and I think it probably lies in the type and magnitude of the risks each takes.

A fighter pilot risks his life on a routine basis; a stock broker risks his and other people's fortunes on a routine basis. The commonality here between these two august professions is the routine, repeated risk-taking. The greater risk, in deference to Maslow's hierarchy, I think must belong to the fighter pilot. He risks his life; the stock broker risks only money. However, in all fairness to the stock broker, it bears remembering that when the stock market crashed in 1929 and fortunes crumbled, many people compounded the tragedy with suicide.

Sometime, I oughtta interview a stock broker or two, to find out if their lives are as full of 'broking stocks' as a fighter pilot's is with flying fighters.

(ref Eccl 93010401)

1013 T. Mike

His name was T. Mike Messett, and T. Mike had the brick
From kicking shit the night before, T. Mike was feeling sick
The weather it was dog-shit; 'twas really quite a day
He didn't want to be the SOF down there at CCK

Colonel Kuni called him in, said, "T. Mike, listen up;
Be sure to keep a close eye on the boys called Haze and Tup
Keep a close eye on the weather and make 'em watch the gas;
If you get my tit in a wringer, you bet I'll have your ass."

T. Mike snapped a smart salute, he belched and scratched his balls
He took a drag from a cigar butt, and he blew it at the walls
He said, "No sweat, Kuni; you can depend on me.
I flew Convair's Delta Dart, and I can fly the F4C!"

'Twas 18 January; the wind was off the Straits
The fog was lurking, low and thick, at the 36 Tacan Gate
Mike said, "No sweat! Launch the fleet; you see I have the brick
The weather never stopped me when I flew the 106!"

Mike began to smell a rat when the Phantoms came back home
It all began to turn to shit at CCK Aerodrome
The guys were low on JP-4; the warning lights were lit
T. Mike said, "Now, listen, guys; don't give the SOF no shit!"

Woody Bryant's hydraulics were tits-up, shot to hell
He said, "I'm gonna land it; I'll take the old BAK-12!"
Jimmy Lewis said, "My generator's quit on me!"
And Acie Brucie called up with, "I've got a BLC!"

T. Mike said, "Now, hold it, guys; I'm gonna get you down;
Haze 61 is low on gas; the world is turning brown.
Heiser's on the downwind; he lost his canopy!"
And as the tears ran down his face, old T. Mike said, "Why me!?"

Woody took the BAK-12, then Jimmy Lewis came in
And Ace had dropped his gear and flaps and landed once again
Haze 61 diverted; he landed long and fast
He heard the angels singing, "Martin Baker saved your ass . . ."

Now T. Mike is reposing in Fighter Pilots' Hell
And every happy hour, they make him ring the bell
He only has to work each time the weather is WOXOF
'Cause T. Mike's new assignment is Satan's Combat SOF

. . . *hero zero* . . . ?   *Dick Jonas*
    They say America needs heroes. That's for damn sure. If it weren't for our soldiers, sailors, airmen and Marines — and our cops and fire fighters — we'd be hero zero.
    Even Rin-Tin-Tin is a son-of-a-bitch.

(ref Eccl 93062001)

1 0 1 4 322FS History Song

In nineteen hundred and forty one, with World War II well begun
They said, "Put on a flight suit son, you're working for the Air Force."

  . . . Air Force . . .

  I was working — pushing throttles, tilting bottles

  Flipping switches, chasing bitches

  I was working for the Air Force . . . YEOW!

In nineteen hundred and forty three, the 322nd came to be
Spitfires climbing to meet the Hun
They didn't stop 'til the job was done

  . . . The Job Was Done . . .

  They were flying — pushing throttles, tilting bottles

  Flipping switches, chasing bitches

  They were flying for the Air Force . . . YEOW!

Prince Bernhards' plan was really sound
He got the squadron off the ground
He didn't give up, he's quite a guy, he literally made ol' Polly fly

  . . . Ol' Polly fly . . .

  He was thinking — clever things, like having wings

  Spinning wheels, making deals

  He was working towards an Air Force . . . YEOW!

In nineteen hundred and seventy seven
Terroists grabbed a train to heaven
Six 104s, so I've heard tell, mach'd those bastards straight to Hell

  . . . Straight to Hell . . .

  They were flying — pushing throttles, tilting bottles

  Flipping switches, chasing bitches

  They were flying for the Air Force . . . YEOW!

Some slogans say, 'Oh just screw it'
Theirs is "Don't Talk — Just Do It"
The planes they fly are really keen
And now they fly the F-Sixteen . . . F-16 . . .
>They are flying — pushing throttles, tilting bottles
>Flipping switches, chasing bitches
>They are flying for the Air Force . . . YEOW!

Air to Ground or Air to Air, Three-two-two does it's share
Blade13 felt mighty fine, when he shot down a MiG-29
>. . . MiG-29 . . .
>He was flying — pushing throttles, tilting bottles
>Flipping switches, chasing bitches
>He was flying for the Air Force . . . YEOW!

What can we say? Hey, they're the best
They've fought the fight, they've stood the test
The Diana's are there, across the way
They're a "bunch of pussies" the Pollys say
>. . . Bunch of pussies . . .
>But they, too, are flying — pushing throttles, tilting bottles
>Flipping switches, chasing bitches
>They were flying for their Air Force . . . YEOW!

From Leeuwarden to Kyrgyzstan, "Hey, who's the Boss?
Yeah, who's the man?" If we shout out, "WHO FUCKS WHO?"
They'll shout back, **"THREE TWO TWO!"**
>**. . . Bunch of Pussies . . .**
>They are flying — pushing throttles, tilting bottles
>Flipping switches, chasing bitches
>They are flying for the Air Force. (Royal Dutch Air Force!)
>**YEOW!!! _ SECOND TO NONE!!!**

. . . don't talk, just do it . . . *Irv LeVine*

Sixty years of proud, faithful, honorable service to one's nation is most laudable and needs to be recognized. The 322nd's birthday celebration allowed Dick and me the opportunity to join with the brave men and women of the Royal Dutch Air Force in a celebration of Celebrations. In order to do a light hearted, slightly whimsical history of the squadron I felt a song needed to be composed. Sixty years of activities and accomplishments that span several wars and periods of unrest and foment is a lot to take on in just a few short verses. The spirit of the men and women of the 322 needed to be felt along with their accomplishments. How better to recognize them for their past accomplishments as well as some of their more recent ones. All this I felt should be done in a manner befitting their squadron slogan: "DON'T TALK! JUST DO IT!" and their "go to Hell" manner and present high level of joie de vivre. Our hats are off to the seamless souls who make the 322nd the flying, fighting machine it has always been and still is today.

Woody & Jimi

Happy hour, Leeuwarden O'Club, Friday night, 13 Jun 2003

. . . don't talk, just do it . . . *Oivind "Igor" Jervan*
    This document is the official approval of the 322 Fighter Squadron's Polly emblem. It is signed by King George R.I. at the College of Arms in 1944.

1015 I've Been Everywhere

Original song by Geoff Mack. Parody lyrics ©1997 Dick Jonas. All rights reserved.

Well, I took off from Ubon in a thick and heavy driving rain
I toted my bombs out to Green Anchor tanker plane
I had this brand new AC riding in the front seat
A guy with six months RTU, before that, a Tweet
He asked me if my counters numbered much more than ten
I said, "Listen, Mac, there ain't no place up there I ain't been!"
>   CHORUS
>   I've been everywhere, Man, I've been everywhere
>   I crossed the mountains bare, Man, I seen the flak-filled air
>   Of SAMs I've had my share, Man, I've been everywhere

I been to Hanoi, Haiphong, Phuc Yen, Yen Bai
Lang Son, Hoa Lac, Phu Tho, Son Tay
Hoa Binh, Nam Dinh, Thai Binh, Bac Ninh
Thai Nguyen, Gia Lam, Viet Tri, Do Son
Thud Ridge, MiG Ridge, Northeast Railroad
Bac Mai, Ninh Giang, Bac Giang, Poo-yeng
>   CHORUS

I been to Sam Neua, Ban Ban, Quang Tri, Son La
Bat Lake, Dong Hoi, Quang Khe, Thanh Hoa
Red Route, Black Route, Blue Route, Purple Route
Channel 97 and the Red and Black River Valley
Land side, water side, down the slide, dang my hide
In town, cross town, up town, down town
>   CHORUS

I been to Taegu, Kwangju, Fuchu, Kunsan
Inchon, Osan, Pusan, Suwon
P-Y Do, Cheju do, Guam, Okinawa
Hachinohe, Morioka, Sendai, Wakkanai
Tachikawa, Itazuke, Niigata, Pohang
Kagoshima, Hiroshima, Ie Shima, hot dang!
CHORUS

I been to Seoul, Kimpo, Honolulu, Wake, Midway
Hong Kong, Bangkok, Baguio, Manila Bay
Hualien, Tainan, Taitung, Keelung
Chiayi, Hsin chu, Kaohsiung, Ping Tung
Saigon, Singapore, Tokyo, Taipei
Taichung city, all night, all day
CHORUS

Geoff Mack

Australian entertainer from Sydney. Wrote the original "I've Been Everywhere," including Australian, U. S., German, and Japanese versions. As of this writing, the song is up to more than two dozen versions by various writers.

1016 Ballad of Jeb Stuart

On a steep and jagged hillside near Mu Gia Pass
Hanging in a parachute, this day is his last
Just another fighter jock, they're mostly all the same
But this one here was different, Jeb Stuart was his name

Jeb was feeling mighty poorly, both his legs was broke
And I could see him hanging there between the puffs of smoke
I told Jeb, "Now, drink some water; Sandy's on the way;
The Jolly Greens are coming in, we'll get you out today."

I could tell that he was hurt much worse than first I thought
'Cause sometimes he just wouldn't answer, then sometimes he'd talk
"Ole Jeb likely needs a doctor," I had said to Crown
And he came back with, "Jolly's got PJs; they'll soon be down."

I held high and kept Jeb talking to me all the while
When I told him, "Here comes Sandy!" I could see him smile
Jeb said, "Listen, Babes, you have ole Sandy watch his stuff;
They got ZPU and small arms; this one's gon' be tough."

Sandy flew right down the valley looking for the sites
He pulled off with battle damage and turned around to fight
Jeb called up and told him, "Sandy! Bring it down again;
The guns are down behind the karst! Now lay your napalm in. . ."

Jeb worked Sandy like a FAC; "Hit twenty meters right!
Watch the small arms on the left!" Then all the guns went quiet

10-33

Jeb was talking low and weaker; time was running out
The guns were down and Jolly's here; but I began to doubt

First the PJs tried to reach him, but it took too long
And I was bingo minus seven; time to head for home
All the way to Wolfpack country, not a word was said
'Cause when the PJ finally reached him, young Jeb Stuart was dead

We rolled out and taxied in and climbed out in the rain
Hoot and Bill and all the boys, they met us at the plane
I told Hoot, "Jeb didn't make it; they got him at the Pass.
And I came home because my bird was running out of gas."

Listen, boys, and hear me good; I want you all to know
That old Jeb died a hero's death, the way we all would go . . .

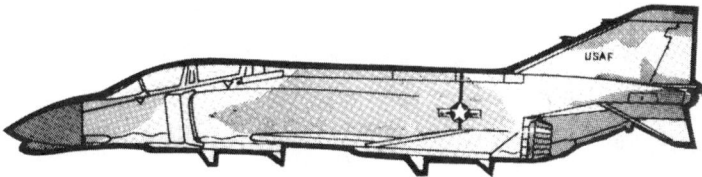

F-4C Phantom II
Scan from Dash One

1017 RBAAB: The Red-Blooded, All-American Boy

I'm an RBAAB and I fly the F-16
It's better than sex and mom's apple pie
It's the neatest little jet you ever seen
It'll kick the shit outta Foxbat, Fishbed, Flogger
What a flying machine
I'm an RBAAB and I fly the F-16

I once trapped at six a Fox-Five-Echo
At seventeen-thousand feet
And he was loaded with twenty-millimeter
And Aim-nine J and P
I just laid a bat-turn down his throat
And I shot him in the two front teeth
And I heard him shout from the fireball
 "Curse you! I just can't stand the heat!"
         . . .So I told him to get the hell outta my kitchen. . .

Had a little friend down in southern Arizona
That flew the Eagle jet
Sent me a letter, said, "Come on down
I got something that you ain't seen yet."
So I kicked my tires and I lit my fire
And over Wickenburg, we met
And in 22 seconds my little friend calls up and says
 "Hey! I wanta change the bet!"
         . . . So I asked him what it felt like to be
                 Number Two . . .

10-35

Now, there ain't no yarn about flying and fighting
That's done without a Tomcat tale
So I took it down to Miramar the 4th of July
I got a buddy there that likes to sail
Now the weather was dog-shit, but we went anyway
The hell with the blooming gale
He never seen me, but I seen him
And I shot a buncha holes in his tail
      . . . Kinda made the fur fly on that Tomcat. . .

Now, if ever Ivan decides to fight
And I just kinda think he will
I may get a chance to show that turkey
What it means to fly and kill
Me and the Lima and the Electric Jet
Are prob'ly gonna fit the bill
We'll run him down from Hell to breakfast
And kick his ass for drill!

I'm an RBAAB and I fly the F-16
It's better than sex and mom's apple pie
It's the neatest little jet you ever seen
It'll kick the shit outta Foxbat, Fishbed, Flogger
What a flying machine
I'm an RBAAB and I fly the F-16

1018 Crack Went the Rifle

The poor boy walks the winding jungle trail
His eyes alert; his mind on the morning mail
      Last sound to reach his ear
      The culmination of all his fears
Crack went the rifle in his hand

Mrs Smith, your son died a hero's death
Defending the way of life we all love best
      I know it's hard to understand
      How his dying will save this land
But statesmen say it's all worth the price

Crack went the rifle in his hand
The leaden bullets raged across the land
      For Jonny Smith from New Orleans
      A gift from a man-made killing machine
Crack went the rifle in his hand

War is such a manly game to play
Makes heroes out of plain men, so they say
      While cultured men in shirts of lace
      Debate the shape of the meeting place
The common man plays hide and seek with death

So come on, boys, don't let your spirits lag
Beware the man who vows to save the flag

After all is said and done

It's you and me that carry the gun

And walk the road to Hell once again

Crack went the rifle in his hand

The leaden bullets raged across the land

For Jonny Smith from New Orleans

A gift from a man-made killing machine

Crack went the rifle in his hand

. . . Crack went the rifle in his hand . . .

Rifle Toter *Dick Jonas*

My first experience with the military was in the Valdosta, Georgia, Army National Guard. It was a mech infantry company, and I served while I went to college. I loved it. Camping out (bivouac) was right up this ol' redneck boy's alley. I shot the M-1 Garand, the M-1919A6 .30 caliber machine gun, the Browning Automatic Rifle (BAR), the Bazooka, and the M-1911 .45 caliber pistol. Some of my most enjoyable days were spent in the Army infantry school at Ft Jackson, South Carolina.

1019   Woody's Song "Polly and 322"

If the shit hits the fan, now here is the plan, this is the squadron to call
We hop in our jets and as fast as it gets
We'll be the ones standing tall
Our guns loaded hot, all the missiles we got
Eager and ready to shoot
We'll do the job, go right for the top like nobody else ever could

CHORUS

We're three-two-two — swing role killers
No triple-A, no SAMs thrill us
If the word is go, we run the show
Polly and Three-Two-Two

Targets high and fast, targets low and slow
If you want 'em splashed, let us know
We hit the gas, and we kick their ass
Polly and Three-Two-Two

Air-to-air far the best, we intercept fast
Them bandits got nowhere to run
They might think they're tougher, but we let them suffer
And finally kill them for fun
Quite stunning we do attack ground targets, too
Who should we fry, tell us, pal
We capture the spot and right on the dot, we blow the fucker to hell

CHORUS

10-39

Woody
Dick Jonas

After Igor and the 322 had invited Irv and me to the celebration, they wanted to know if we could sing Woody's song. I've since learned that the squadron had been singing the thing for a decade. Not knowing that, I proceeded to put my own spin on it and began inventing a tune. The way the muse hummed the note sequence required that I take a liberty or two with the lyrics.

I hope Woody will forgive me that.

Anyway, I'm truly delighted to have shared song-writing chores with a shit-hot Dutch fighter pilot. I think it will add a nice flavor to my resumè.

Thanks, Woody!

Dick & Woody

Happy hour, Leeuwarden O'Club, Friday night, 13 Jun 2003

1020 Swamp Fox

I'm a Swamp Fox; I got my gun cocked
I'm meaner than hell in the air or in the chocks
I'm a Triple-T-E-Double-M-F-K, I am

    I keep the Carolina skies pretty safe for democracy .
    And the United States of America depends on me
I got a tough machine, don't you know what I mean
A neat little jet they call the F-16
It'll out-fly any other flying machine, by damn

    It'll kick a MiG-23's ass all over the sky
    And Ivan ain't got a single thing that it won't out-fly
I've been to Norway; I went with Bob Gray
We done a lotta living every night and day
And everybody over there said we knew the meaning of class

    The northern Europeans kinda like the way I do my thing
    The way I fly my jet; the way that I dance and sing
I've been to River Street with the SCANG elite
There ain't a lotta places that's nearly this neat
And even if there is, well I don't give a big rat's ass

    Vegas ain't never gonna ever be the same again
    At Gunsmoke, we kicked a lotta ass with a few good men
I'm a Swamp Fox; and, I'm a Gamecock
I'm meaner than hell in the air or in the chocks
I'm a Triple-T-E-Double-M-F-K, I am

The guys from the Coonass Militia, well they better watch out

We'll show 'em who's the boss, and there ain't gonna

be no doubt

I'm a Swamp Fox; I got my gun cocked

I'm meaner than hell in the air or in the chocks

I'm a Triple-T-E-Double-M-F-K, I am

    ... I'm a Triple-T-E-Double-M-F-K, I am

Swamp Fox! . . . Swamp Fox! . . . Swamp Fox! . . . Yeh-h-h . . .

Wha-a-a-t . . . ?　　　　　　　　　　　　　　　　　*Dick Jonas*

    I expect you figured out right away that, on the CD, we left out the last verse about the Coonass Militia — ?

    I can't *believe* we did that! Anyhoo, here are *all* the words. Knock yourself out . . .

Swamp Fox

157FS, 169FG, South Carolina Air National Guard

1021 322FS Fight Song

If you ask us who the hell we are, we'll give it straight to you
We're the the flying Jolly Pollys, the fighting three-two-two

You can bet we're rough and ready, smooth as a summer breeze
Don't stand up or give us guff, and if you ask, say please

We fly the mighty F-16, we fly it quite a bit
We'll set you up and shoot you down, 'cause we don't give a shit

So, now you know just who we are, yeah, we've got balls of brass
If you don't like our little song, why you can kiss our ass

You asked us who the hell we are, we gave it straight to you
We're the flyin'-fightin' best there is
WE'RE THE FIGHTING THREE TWO TWO! . . . **RAH!**

. . . the fighting three-two-two . . .   *Irv LeVine*

Every hard drinking group needs and deserves a song they can sing together — usually at the top of their lubricated lungs. An easy tune with easy, expressive words — words that can be memorized and shouted out. You can't be around pilots like those we found at the Royal Dutch 322nd Fighter Squadron without realizing their pent up energy has to have some outlet. It might not be a politically correct outlet but if it serves the purpose then in its own way it is politically correct.

The 322nd pilots are singers, as well as lovers and fighters. I tried to emphasize both the former and the latter (they can prove the median on their own) and to give them a chance to say it with this little ditty, if they couldn't find a better way to let go of some of that pent up energy.

Why they're the best   *Dick Jonas*

Igor, the Norwegian exchange jock with the Pollies, was the mover and shaker who brought us all together at Leeuwarden. He and the other jocks deserve a lot of credit for one helluva fine soiree.

Just so you'll know, the engine which powers Igor is pictured below. Pronounce her name "Yets-kuh."

Jetske
Mrs "Igor"

10-44

1022 Aye-Yi-Yi-Yi

Author unknown. Air Force traditional. Arr ©2003 Dick Jonas and Irv LeVine.

Aye-yi-yi-yi, your mother eats batshit off cave walls
I'll sing you another verse that's worse than the other verse
And waltz me around by my willy

There once was a fellow from Boston, who bought himself
a little Austin
There was room for his ass and a gallon of gas
But his balls hung out and he lost 'em

Aye-yi-yi-yi, your sister does squat thrusts on fire plugs
I'll sing you another verse that's worse than the other verse
And waltz me around by my willy

There once was a young man from Brighton, remarked to his girl,
"Its a tight one!"
She said, "Shut your face; you got it in the wrong place
And there's plenty of room in the right one!"

Aye-yi-yi-yi, your sister eats moose cum off pine cones
I'll sing you another verse that's worse than the other verse
And waltz me around by my willy

There once was this guy from Kildare, who was screwing his wife
on the stair
The bannister broke, so he doubled his stroke
And finished her off in mid-air

Aye-yi-yi-yi, in China they do it for chile
I'll sing you another verse that's worse than the other verse
And waltz me around by my willy

There once was a lady from Trask, she had a magnificent ass
Not pretty and pink as you probably think
It was gray, had long ears, and ate grass

Aye-yi-yi-yi, your mother eats batshit off fire plugs
I'll sing you another verse that's worse than the other verse
And waltz me around by my willy
In the Garden of Eden sat Adam, stroking the butt of his madam
His chuckled with mirth, for he knew on this Earth
There were only two balls, and he had 'em
    Aye-yi-yi-yi, in China they do it for rice wine
    I'll sing you another verse that's worse than the other verse
    And waltz me around by my willy
There once was a young man from Florida, who liked his friend's wife
    so he borrowed her
He said with surprise as he opened her thighs
"That ain't no crotch; that's a corridor!"
    Aye-yi-yi-yi, your sister eats pine shit off moose cones
    I'll sing you another verse that's worse than the other verse
    And waltz me around by my willy
An Argentine gaucho named Bruno, said sex is one thing I do know
All women are fine, and the sheep is devine
But a llama is numero uno
    Aye-yi-yi-yi, in Japan they do it for anything
    I'll sing you another verse that's worse than the other verse
    And waltz me around by my willy
There once was a young lady from Ransom, who got it three times
    in a hansom
When she cried for more, a voice from the floor
Said, "My name is Simpson, not Samson!"
    Aye-yi-yi-yi, (. . . *inane laughter . . .*)
    I'll sing you another verse that's worse than the other verse
    And waltz me around by my willy

There once was a girl from Hoboken, who claimed that her cherry
    got broken
From riding her bike on a cobblestone pike
But it really got broken from pokin'

    Aye-yi-yi-yi, your sister does squat thrusts on fire plugs
    I'll sing you another verse that's worse than the other verse
    And waltz me around by my willy

There once was this cat named Magruder, who wooed this nude
    in Bermuda
She thought it crude to be wooed in the nude
But Magruder was cruder, he screwed her

    Aye-yi-yi-yi, your mother swims after troop ships
        (and catches 'em!)
    I'll sing you another verse that's worse than the other verse
    And waltz me around by my willy

A Dirty One
Irv LeVine

Some songs like this one have been around for all too many wars, police actions, incidents, accidents and any other 'dent' you can think of. Some will say the verses are too risque, and others will say they're downright dirty.

However, most verses are clever and will tickle your funny bone, and you'll find yourself looking forward to hearing the next verse right along with everyone else — especially after you've had a few adult beverages. Here' s a song where everyone can sing along and everyone is invited to add a verse or six. A more rollicking bit of nonsense fun I've never had . . . and the ladies all laugh the hardest.

Leeuwarden train station

Ruud Heinen's L-39

10-46.2

1023 Banana Valley

Just go on down to Banana Valley, go on down and meet your fate
Just go on down to Banana Valley
But when you go down, down, down you better learn to hate

Well, I got friends in Banana Valley, I got friends that learned too late
I got friends in Banana Valley
They went down, down, down 'cause they did not hate

There's snakes in the weeds in Banana Valley
Them snakes in the weeds know how to hate
Them snakes in the weeds in Banana Valley
They go down, down, down and there they wait

Well, I heard all about Banana Valley
      how fighting them snakes could be so great
So much fun in Banana Valley
Gotta go down, down, down and investigate

Two weeks ago in Banana Valley
      two of my friends killed one of them snakes
Two weeks ago in Banana Valley
They went down, down, down to attend a wake

So go one down to Banana Valley, go on down and meet your fate
Just go on down to Banana Valley
But when you go down, down, down you better learn to hate

Play list   *Dick Jonas*

I was somewhat surprised at which of the Vietnam era songs the 322 guys wanted to hear. This one was high on the list, as was *Jeb Stuart.* I've always liked *Banana Valley* because the story about ". . . two of my friends . . . " is true. See *RBAAB*, page 1-32.

I used to have trouble getting through *Jeb Stuart* without puddling up, until I'd sung it a few thousand times. It, too, is a true story, and a very sad one, as well.

But, I think the lesson I learn here is that warriors who are tough as nails on the outside have human hearts inside, and intellect which responds to what is real.

MiG-17

A snake from the weeds.

1024 Royal Goddam Dutch

The Royal goddam Dutch, they're real good at fighting and such
They'll chase you, they'll hound you until they surround you
      The Royal goddam Dutch

They're meaner than Satan himself, they got lotsa tricks on the shelf
In Spitfires and Starfighters, Hawkers and Vipers
      I don't think they need any help

They came here from 'way cross the sea, to party with Irving and me
They do lots of braggin' 'bout their honey wagon
      Just watch them and you will see

The Royal goddam Dutch, they're real good at flying and such
But they ain't got no sense, not even the prince
      The Royal goddam Dutch

Watch out for the Royal Dutch, they're nice guys but not very much
They'll catch you not lookin' and piss in your cookin'
      Beware of the Royal Dutch

I'm happy to call them my friend, we're brothers under the skin
The enemy's fast, but we'll kick his ass
      The brotherhood never will end

There go the Royal Dutch, there go the Royal Dutch
The memories are hazy, those bastards are crazy
      There go the Royal Dutch

The Royal goddam Dutch, they're real good at fighting and such

They'll chase you, they'll hound you and then they will pound you

The Royal goddam Dutch

Brothers   *Dick Jonas*

The third verse makes more sense if you know that the 322 came to the States for an exercise a couple of weeks before the celebration at Leeuwarden. We hooked up in San Diego for a dress rehearsal.

I was not surprised to find that Dutch fighter pilots are not much different from American figihter pilots. Their aviator mien and vernacular, both in the air and at the bar, is pretty much the same as ours. Brothers under the skin we are.

322 Fighter Squadron

How's your Dutch? It says, "Don't talk; just act."

10-50

11

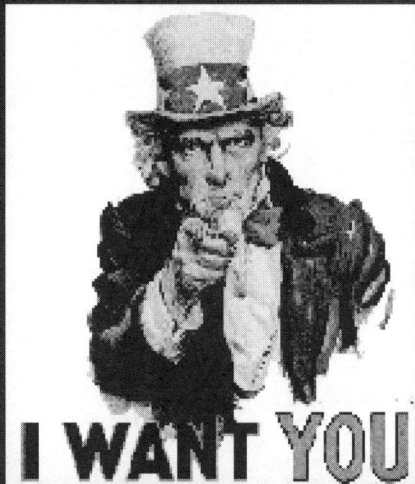

Come and Join the Air Force

Irv
LeVine

Dick
Jonas

Chip
Dockery

Toby
Hughes

I WANT YOU

This album is dedicated to the memory of
James Patterson "Bull" Durham
with the profoundest affection, admiration, and respect.

EROSONIC

Album Eleven

The Patriarchy

EROSONIC
Recording
Session
Oct 2004

Toby

Dick

Chip

Emmit
(the musician)

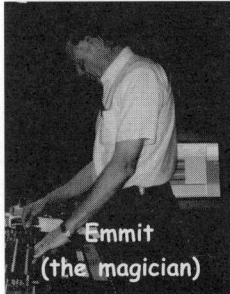
Emmit
(the magician)

Irv - Sally - Mary

1101 Missing Man

"Twenty-one guns, stars and stripes
An eye full of tears and a heart full of pride
When you hear that distant bugle play
Another old soldier fades away
Another old soldier fades away
Another old soldier fades away
Another old soldier fades away."

. . . Bull Durham and the Heard, 'Another Old Soldier Fades Away.'

As we gather to sing our songs again, there's an empty space in our ranks. The songs in this collection are dedicated to the memory of Bull, our friend and colleague, now on his flight with the angels. Bull was the Elder Statesman of this group of vets who tell our stories in song, having served his country in three wars, two hot, and one cold. He was big, loud, boisterous, bawdy, rowdy, rough around the edges, a true patriot, a hell-raiser and a helluva musician. Just our kind of guy. He could con you with the straightest of faces, but the twinkle in his eye always gave him away. He was a spellbinder. No matter how many times you had heard the story or the joke he was telling, you listened again. With his band, Bull entertained and delighted audiences wherever they performed. With our group, he provided, in addition to his incredible musical contributions, humor, folk wisdom, and true historical perspective. There are so many other things that can be said about the man, but others' words cannot describe Bull nearly so well as do his own.

(Excerpt from 'Austin City Limits'):

"My name is James Patterson Durham, and I was born in Mt. Tabor, Kentucky, and I'm famous for a lot of things. I've picked cotton, I've plucked chickens, I've shucked corn, I play a guitar and sing; when I walk down the streets of Nashville they say 'there goes the best cotton pickin' chicken pluckin' corn shuckin' guitar playin' singer in the whole world.'"

And so he was. We miss our friend, but it's only for a while. For in the words of another song that he loved, 'We'll all meet at that final great reunion, and fly with angels, out beyond the stars.'

Three's out!

Bull

1102 Come and Join the Air Force

Author unknown. Air Force traditional. Arrangement ©2005 Dick Jonas. All rights reserved.

Come and join the Air Force, we're a happy band they say
We never do a lick of work, just fly around all day
While others work or study hard and soon grow old and blind
We take the air without a care and you will never mind

> CHORUS
> You'll never mind, you'll never mind
> Come and join the Air Force and you will never mind

Promotions come upon you as fast as you desire
You're riding on a gravy train when you're an Air Force flyer
But just when you're about to be a general you will find
The engine coughs, the wings fall off, but you will never mind
> CHORUS

One day you'll loop and spin her and with an awful tear
You'll find yourself without your wings, but you will never care
'Cause in about two minutes more another pair you'll find
You'll fly with Pete and angels sweet, and you will never mind
> CHORUS

You're flying across the ocean when you hear the engine spit
You see your prop come to a stop, the goddam motor's quit
The ship won't float, you cannot swim, the shore is far behind
You'll be a dish for crabs and fish, but you will never mind
> CHORUS

11-5

I'm flying in my '86 along the Yalu shore

I'm loyal to the Air Force, but rotten to the core

I've only got one engine, and should that bastard quit

It'll be up there all by itself, 'cause I will shit and git!

CHORUS

Maybe you'll ride the gravy train in administrative work

Let other guys light up the skies, why should you be a jerk?

You'll meet that chair-borne colonel to whom you've been assigned

With your nose in place (and not on your face) but, you

will never mind

CHORUS

. . . a happy band . . .   *Dick Jonas*
Thinking about the Indians . . .
America has lots of war memorials: WWI; WWII; Vietnam; Korea . . . TONS of Civil War memorials.
To my knowledge, there's no memorial for the veterans of the Indian Wars. And I don't mean veterans of European descent, I mean the Northwestern Hemispherian veterans — the Indians who died in battle defending their homeland.
The term "Indian" is out these days; it's been replaced by "Native American." I can't imagine that the Cherokees and the Creeks and the Shoshones and the Nez Perce and the Sioux and the Apaches and the others appreciate being named after an Italian sailor, anymore than they do being named after a south Asian race. It was all a big mistake. It happened because Chris Columbus, a Genoese sailor who was a poor navigator, got lost.
Amerigo Vespucci was an Italian.
What if our country were named the United States of Vespucci? The Vespuccian Air Force. "I am a Vespuccian fighter pilot." Yucchhhh!!! Doesn't EVEN roll off the tongue.
I'll bet the Indians feel the same way about "Indian" and "Native American."
Arapaho. Mohawk. Seminole. Papago. Anasazi. Hopi. Navajo. Such . . . class. Such dignity. Such identity.
"Howdy, Ma'am. Mind if a Cheyenne skywarrior buys you a drink?"
(ref Eccl 93082218)

1103 Co-Pilot's Lament

Author unknown. Air Force traditional. Arrangement ©2005 Dick Jonas. All rights reserved.

Oh, I'm the co-pilot, I sit on the right
I'm thinking, courageous, and wonderfully bright
My job is rememb'ring what the captain forgets
And I never talk back, so I have no regrets

     I'm a lousy co-pilot and a long way from home

I fill out the form one and study the weather
Handle the gear and I stand by to feather
I make out his mail forms, I hire his whores
And fly this old crate to the tune of his snores

     I'm a lousy co-pilot and a long way from home

I make out the flight plan according to Hoyle
Take all the readings, and I check the oil
Hustle out the crew for the midnight alarm
And fly through the fog while he sleeps on my arm

     I'm a lousy co-pilot and a long way from home

I treat him to coffee, I keep him in smokes
I laugh at his corn and his horrible jokes
And once in a while when his landings are rusty
I come through with "Yessirree, Captain, it's gusty!"

     I'm a lousy co-pilot and a long way from home

All in all I'm commissioned a general stooge

I sit on the right of this high-flying Scrooge

Someday I'll make captain and then I'll be blessed

I'll give my poor tongue one long hell of a rest

I'm a lousy co-pilot and a long way from home

... Someday I'll make captain ... *Dick Jonas*

I had two frightening brushes with the role of co-pilot. I was a back seat pilot in the F-4, then when I retired from the Air Force, I flew with an airline long enough to find out I was *not* meant to fly airliners. The trouble with the pit (F-4 back seat) was you couldn't see forward, and you couldn't select afterburner with the throttles. The trouble with an airliner right seat was all that time away from my home and favorite toys. Plus, in those days, you were going to be a co-pilot for a long, long time before you ever made captain.

I am the typical fighter pilot control freak. I cannot stand not being the boss on my airplane.

Curtiss C-46

Flew the Hump and other adventurous routes.

1104 Bucaneers

Buccaneers, Buccaneers
We're a cut-and-half-or-two above our peers
We're the fighting four-two-eight
And our mamas think we're great
We're the shit-hot, flying, fighting Buccaneers

We've been challenged by the Navy and Marines
Beat the pants off Phantom jets and F-14s
Showed those guys what flyin' and fightin' really means
And they shudder in their boots at Buccaneers

Buccaneers, Buccaneers
We're a cut-and-half-or-two above our peers
We're the best on this air patch
The F-16 ain't got no match
We're the combat, flying, fighting Buccaneers

F-5Es and the mighty Eagle jets
They surmise that what they see is what they gets
And they gamble, but they always lose their bets
To the steely-eyed and deadly Buccaneers

Buccaneers, Buccaneers
We're a cut-and-half-or-two above our peers
With it's missiles and it's gun, the Viper jet's a lot of fun
And we're proud to be the fighting Buccaneers

Now old Ivan has the power and the might

And his missiles, guns and jets are outta sight

But we'll show him what it means to fly and fight

And we'll win 'cause we're the mighty Buccaneers

Buccaneers, Buccaneers

We're a cut-and-half-or-two above our peers

We're the best in the USA, and we prove it every day

We're the shit-hot, flying, fighting Buccaneers

The Bucs   *Dick Jonas*

I spent close onto four years in the 474th TFW at Nellis in the late 70s - early 80s. Part of the time I was a wing weenie in the weapons and tactics shop, assigned there out of the 428th Squadron. At one time or another, I was attached for flying to both the other two outfits in the Wing. My last duty in the 474th was Assistant Ops Officer in the 428th. The happiest time of my life there was flying the line with the Buccaneers.

I debuted this song at a party thrown by Gen Bill Creech at HQ TAC, Langley AFB, Virginia, in the early '80s.

1105   ORI

I hear that klaxon blowing, somebody's rung the bell
I climb into my flight suit, my body's just a shell
'Cause it's early Monday morning with a clear blue sky
And the PACAF toads are coming with the ORI

They told me Friday evening, no sweat, just go on home
It couldn't be next Monday, so I hung up the phone
I packed up my Volkswagen, wife and kids and all
And I headed for Okuma to have myself a ball

I motored up through Nago, the sea breeze in my face
There ain't no cause for worry in such a lovely place
So I broke out a bottle and partied all night long
It was 0400 Monday when I got back home

My head just hit the pillow, my wife had said good night
The whistle started blowing as I put out the light
I must be having nightmares, there must be some mistake
And now I'm trying to preflight, but I can't stay awake

It's 1500 broken, the weather's moving in
The crosswind's getting stronger, but here we go again
They launched the force at seven, in a driving rain
It feels just like a typhoon is sweeping through my brain

Somebody up there likes me, my bird came back OR

I got my bombs on target and the Old Man bought the bar

He told us all a secret, a twinkle in his eye

He said, "I'd rather face a typhoon than bust an ORI!"

Speaking of typhoons   *Dick Jonas*

In WestPac during typhoon season, it was customary to evac the airplanes from Okinawa if those things got too close. Nifty, unscheduled TDY to exotic places like Yokota, Japan, or Clark Air Base in the Philippines, or to Osan or Kunsan, ROK. But, we were subject to a small guilt trip. You see, the families didn't get evacked; they had to stay on Oki and brave the storm's fury. It seemed to me that typhoons were more destructive than the hurricanes I remembered from my youth in Florida. Although; in 2004 and 2005, Caribbean hurricanes joined the big leagues.

So, the families stayed behind while we went off to bask in calm and comfort.

While I was at Kadena, there was one typhoon — we didn't evac for this one — which came up the east side of the island about 60 miles out. Over the next few days, it made a complete 360° circle around Okinawa, remaining about 60 miles out the whole time. It was like the weather gods were doing a recce mission.

While we did get our share of ORIs and other PACAF instigated inspections, this song is more fighter pilot fiction. I'm sure had the balloon gone up, though, one measly typhoon would not have stopped us from executing the mission.

F-4E

Desert Storm era. At Kadena, we had Vietnam era C models.

1106   Bill Anders

His name is Bill Anders, a daring young man
If it needs flying, Bill Anders can
He came out of Squid School and then pretty soon
Young William Anders, flew off to the moon!

Born in Hong Kong, far over the sea
Looked up at the sky, and said, "That's for me."
Signed up with the Air Force to hedge all his bets
Bill got his wish and was soon flying jets

In the F-89 and the F-101
He chased Russian bombers 'neath a cold northern sun
He's flown it all — jets, rockets, and props
And some even tell me that he's flown wop-wops!

He got his chance in 1963
He learned how to fly the LLTV
The moon was the mission for Bill and his crew
They wanted to find out just what he could do

1968, just about Christmastime
The rocket fired up and it started its climb
The engines were roaring a thunderous tune
Bill, Frank, and Jimmy were off to the moon!

𝄞 ⚘ ☙ ❧ ❧ ☙ ⊙

They watched it roll by 98 miles below
They saw the earth rise, what a wonderful show!
Read from the Good Book to the people on earth
And midwifed the moment of the new frontier's birth

Astronaut, statesman, and businessman, too
There just ain't nothing Bill Anders can't do
He's a wonderful guy, and I'm glad he's my friend
The country owes much to this man among men

You'll find him at Reno or some other air patch
Flying Valhalla or the big Wampus Cat
On the wing of an A-10 or another hot jet
Bill just won't quit, he's still flying yet
       Bill Anders won't quit, he's still flying yet

Bill   *Greg Anders*

One of the earliest memories in my life was going out to Ellington AFB and watching my Dad fly the Lunar Landing Training Vehicle (LLTV). I was 4 or 5 and I thought it was cool. Noisy, but cool. At the age of six I remember being stopped midstream in a rousing game of tag so I could watch our brand new <u>color</u> TV and see my Dad take off in a Saturn V. Again, I thought it was cool and I imagine my comment to my friends as I walked away was something along the lines of "Did you see that! Isn't color TV cool!" At that age, I cannot be accused of having 'the big picture.' I thought everybody's dad was an astronaut. I was more excited at meeting the fireman's son; his dad got to drive a cool truck at work.

Bill was doing what all fighter pilots do, working to fly the fastest and hottest rig out there. And boy did he! Even the Habu drivers stop talking speed when the 25,000 mph guy walks in the room!

One of the most impressive things to me about Bill is the fact that he was the first to circle the moon, took the greatest picture of the 20th century — "Earthrise" — and yet he continued to press on with his life, putting in just as much, if not more, effort to fulfill his responsibilities. He still had higher goals for himself. And always, there was the goal to fly hot iron.

To that end, when Bill left the astronaut corps to be Executive Secretary for the National Aeronautics and Space Council, he said he'd do it as long as he could keep his "union card" current. So he was authorized to maintain qual in NASA T-38's. When he was appointed to the Atomic Energy Commission, he maintained qual in a T-38. When he was Chairman of the Nuclear Regulatory Commission, he maintained qual in the T-38. When he was Ambassador to Norway, he maintained qual in a T-38. As always, work was a means to an end, and the end was flying.

As Chairman of General Dynamics, he was one of the night test pilots for the Viper's night systems. Why night? Every night sortie profile was flown in its entirety during the day, prior to being flown at night, so Bill could count on two sorties.

In "retirement" (believe me, Bill doesn't retire), he filled that extra time with flying. Soon he was flying what is arguably the world's greatest fighter aircraft of all time (especially when measured by the standard of "pilot lust to fly her"): the P-51 Mustang. He enjoyed that, but also drew a great deal of pleasure from the world of bi-planes, tail-draggers, gliders and even the occasional "whop-whopping" helicopter.

Today, Bill is preserving his country's heritage. He established the Heritage Flight Museum (www.heritageflight.org) to honor veterans and preserve some of the stories and vehicles that made this country what it is today. He wants stories told by the veterans that were there, not by the historians writing about the vets that were there. Two hundred years from now, there will be "Earthrise" and, hopefully, his museum. He was probably still thinking longer term than that, even.

Apollo 8
Apollo 8 was the first manned launch of the Saturn V launch vehicle. In this photo, each of the 5 F1 engines is producing 1.5 million pounds of thrust. The rocket weighed 6 million pounds and was 365 feet tall. It accelerated the capsule to a speed of 35000 ft/sec.

11-14.2

1107   Sher-Babes

Leading the flight north to Khe Sanh, on the thirty third day of the fight
In a red tailed F 4 he called Sher Babes
He flew through the dawn's early light
On Yellow the tanker was waiting,he dropped off just north of the track
Letting down heading two niner zero, and trying to contact the FAC

> Go, Sher Babes, go, down through the blue
> Go, Sher Babes, go, COVEY's waiting for you

COVEY has spotted a truck park, there's NVA, ammo, and guns
Come nightfall they'll slip through the mountains
And zap the Marines at Khe Sanh
The FAC's mark is dead on the target
And Sher Babes is cleared for her run
Starting her long screaming dive now, out of the fast rising sun

> Go, Sher Babes, go, down toward Route Nine
> Go, Sher Babes, go, buy the Gyrenes some time

Then as he pulled off the bomb run
He felt Sher Babes shudder and groan
Saw lights on and gauges unwinding
The guns on the hills had struck home

He's got to get back to the water, but it's eighty five miles to the beach
The left engine's gone, but she's climbing
And safety just might be in reach

"Go, Sher Babes, go," is the prayer that he sang
"Go, Sher Babes, go. We just might make Danang."

His wingman has joined up and checked him
And quietly gives him the call
Ol' Sher Babes is shot all to pieces
And shouldn't be flying at all
The right engine's starting to go now, and how long she'll last he don't know
Into the clouds at six thousand, with twenty five miles still to go

Go, Sher Babes, go, down toward the shore
Go, Sher Babes, go, just a little bit more

She's giving him more than she's got now
With a half mile to go 'fore she's down
One last, loving surge o'er the threshold
She dies as her wheels touch the ground
The crash trucks roar out on the runway
And lay down their blanket of foam
He breathes a short prayer of thanksgiving
For the Lady that's brought him back home

Go, Sher Babes, go; that was the word
Go, Sher Babes, go; you're one hell of a bird

And now your war's over, your battle flag furled
But oh, Sher Babes, oh, you're a beautiful girl

Sher-Babes   *Toby Hughes*

From *What The Captain Means: A Song of the In-Country Air War*
©2005   William F. "Toby" Hughes

The incident related in this song could not possibly have happened. Keep telling yourself that. Keep telling yourself that airplanes are only machines, made of metal and rubber and glass. They cannot think. They are incapable of independent action, being limited by the engineer's design to those characteristics he deems they should have. Airplanes have no soul; they can neither love nor respond to love. They are inanimate objects.

Now. Turn off the computer and let's talk about airplanes. Those to whom descendants of the Wright Flyer are or were a way of life will tell you that in no way is an airplane "just a machine." They may tell you, in all sincerity, that an airplane is not a machine in any way at all. Who that knows airplanes can look at one and not sense its vital essence? The F-100 sitting on the ramp was an open mouthed predator; the F-4 in a low angle bomb pass, a charging rhinoceros. The F-105, diving through the flak bursts over the Doumer Bridge, was a malevolent hornet, its stinger bared. The F-15 is an eagle in more than just its name; the F-16 a pissed off hummingbird, small, agile, and deadly. An earlier generation remembers the P-51, a sleek greyhound straining at the leash, and a brawling Pier Six bully called the P-47. And if you flew anything made by Mitsubishi, and spent time over China in the early days, visions of the shark toothed P-40 still awaken memories of something infinitely more than metal and rubber and glass.

Who that has flown has not at some time coaxed out just a little more than the designer put in? Who has not cursed his fate for being scheduled for a check flight in "Triple Deuce," or blessed it for drawing "Lucky Sevens" for a combat mission that had even the weather briefer scared?

Who has not known those birds with their own personalities, be they good or evil? One thing we learned in six wars in the air is that combat can bring out the good or bad in an airplane, and in that respect, the machine emulates the man.

Yes, he who believes that airplanes are only machines does not know airplanes, and something is missing from his life.

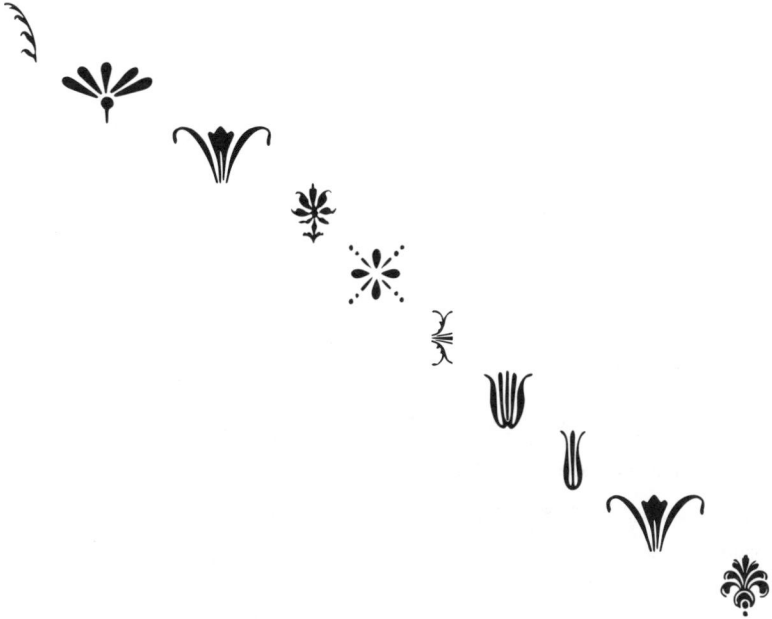

1108 GIB

I came out of Willy Air Patch with my new wings on my chest
Left the student life behind me, gonna fly now with the best
My orders were to fighters and they filled my heart with glee
So I headed south to Tucson where I'd fly the F 4C

I rolled into Davis Monthan and the first man that I saw
Was a big hard drinkin' captain with his elbows on the bar
As he breathed upon my gold bars and I watched them turn to green
Says he's gonna be my AC, says we're gonna be a team

    When I asked him how much fighter time
        his records had to show
    Said he had four years in ATC, there's nothin' he don't know
    But it didn't take me long to learn the frightening life I'd found
    And for seven months I let him hurl my body at the ground

With our training finally over we set out for SEA
To the sunny, sandy airbase on the shores of Cam Ranh Bay
He walked up to our commander, poked an elbow in his rib,
And he said, "I'm Cap'n Hotstick and this wienie here's my GIB."

When we started flying combat, I began to earn my pay
As this clown I called my AC tried to kill me once a day
Droppin' bombs while half inverted, strafin' down among the trees
Comin' off of every target pullin' six or seven g's

But at night around the bar when all the war tales
       they were spun
I'd listen to my AC tell of wondrous deeds he'd done
And I'd wonder just how many more GIBs like me
       that there are
Sittin' silently and listening how their ACs won the war

And when the tour was over and we left that foreign land
As we started on our separate ways he stopped and shook my hand
He said, "You were a good GIB." Then he left, and I was sad
And thought then, to myself, he really wasn't all that bad

'Cause I thought of all the times I didn't know just what to do
When with tricks I didn't understand he'd always pull us through
And one thing became apparent, and the lesson I did heed
Experience is priceless, got to follow 'fore you lead

      'Cause I know now just how green I was and why
          I'm thankful for
The things I learned from this good friend who
          brought me through the war
And I sometimes think I'd like to see him poke the boss's rib
And hear him say, just one more time,
          "This wienie here's my GIB."

The Back Seat Blues   *Toby Hughes*
From *What The Captain Means: A Song of the In-Country Air War*
©2005 William F. "Toby" Hughes

In any two place airplane there has to be one crew member whose primary job is something other than flying the plane. In some aircraft they were called Scope Dopes, in others, PSOs, or maybe just co pilots. In the F 4, at that time, they were called GIBs, an acronym for Guy in Back.

Most GIBs in the war then were lieutenants fresh out of pilot training, in their first operational assignment. They were eager young pilots, itching for a chance to fly, confined by the assignment system to riding the back seat, operating radars and inertials. The Aircraft Commanders got the stick time and the credit, the latter not always deservedly. It was a weary, frustrating job.

It could also be a frightening one. To understand what it was like, imagine yourself strapped in a box, measuring approximately 3 x 3 x 4 feet. Elevate the box to ten thousand feet above the ground, set it in a 45 degree angle of dive and let it drop. Put thrusters on the rear of the box to accelerate it to nearly 500 miles per hour. Have the box not under your control, but in the hands of a man who up until a month or so ago was a total stranger, with whose skills at handling the box you are not yet quite comfortable. Make it dark outside, so you can't see where the box is going. Now throw in some clouds, and put a map in your lap that says there are high mountains all around you. Finally, put a large number of people on the ground, all with guns and a pathological hatred of boxes. Get the picture?

Only if you've done it can you fully understand why the GIBs bitched so much. They earned their right to do that. They also saved some lives. How many ACs are alive today because of their GIBs, there's no way to ever know. The GIBs don't want to talk about it; the ACs don't want to think about it.

A GIB could bad mouth an AC, but usually only his own.

"Old Hamfist almost did us in today!"

"Honest to God, he presses like that one more time, I'm takin' the stick!"

"That ZPU was goin' right over the wing and I don't think the blind sumbitch ever even *saw* it!"

"They were on us like a fat man on a shitter and I had to *tell* him to jink!"

It always seemed a little worse from the box.

The days of the GIB, as we knew him, are over. Specially trained Weapons Systems Officers replaced pilots in the back seat of the F 4. The airplane itself is gone from the active inventory, just a memory of times past. The WSOs did a good job, and their presence freed the pilots to do what they were trained to do, fly. It was a better deal for all concerned. But let us not let the era pass without a salute to that special bunch of hell raisers who fought the war four feet in trail, the GIBs.

To every man who ever rode the back seat, especially Rich Maki, who got a little older in mine, and Colonel Don Lynch, Patron Saint of All The GIBs, this song is dedicated.

Pay attention, guys, you might recognize someone you know.

" . . . The boom is above me, the gashole's behind . . .

(ref page 7-8, this book)

1109   Delta Dawn

The roar of mighty engines splits the morning
On shafts of fire the fighters climb away
The eastern sky's ablaze with light of dawning
For men who fly and fight another day

The sky above the coast is washed in sunlight
The sea is dark as day breaks on the land
The vast and flooded delta's fertile grandeur
Reminds us of how small the works of man

> From twenty thousand feet the land is peaceful
> With the beauty God meant the world to be
> The morning mist, the sparkling silver sunlight
> On the Mekong, flowing gently to the sea

In the spell of this high deep blue enchantment
And the beauty of this lovely verdant land,
How far away the pain, the tears and heartbreak
Of man's cruel inhumanity to man

How long must we endure the bonds of hatred
How long must we heed the call of Mars
How long before all men can live together
How long to bind the wounds and heal the scars

The soldier prays for peace more than all others
For he must bear the deepest wounds of war
Lord, take our hand and lead us through the midnight
To the shining promise of Your morning star

Lord, take our hand and lead us through the midnight
To the shining promise of Your morning star

In the Eye Of the Beholder   *Toby Hughes*
From *What The Captain Means: A Song of the In-Country Air War*
©2005 William F. "Toby" Hughes
    There are many vivid memories of that year. Memories of
fire and rain and fright and sand and sky and death and blue-
green water on pure white beaches and round-eyed nurses and
party hooches and lobster and baked potatoes at 4:00 in the
morning and sorting through friends' personal effects and writing
letters and getting letters and not getting letters and poker
games and AFVN and ARVN and NVA and ZPU and ZSU-23
and Tally Ho at night and Bat Lake at any time and weekends
in Bangkok and R & R with Sher-Babes in Honolulu and armed
recce with Rich in Route Pack One and too much whiskey and not
enough music and so much more that has faded from the memory
of what we all were. But there is one memory that still burns
bright, a memory of a moment so brief, yet so intense that it de-
fies an old man's forgetfulness.
    Scheduled for an early morning mission down into the
Mekong delta, we took off just as the first hint of dawn lightened
the sky above the sea to the east. As we climbed to altitude, we
caught the rising sun, although the earth below was still dark.
As the flight progressed, features on the land below began to
emerge, and I was suddenly and inexplicably struck with the
thought of how beautiful this land was from high above. The ugli-
ness of the war below was, for a brief time, upstaged by the
beauty of God's creation. The river delta seemed to stretch across
forever, the rising sun painting the landscape below from a pal-
ette of green and silver and gold, the sky above with a surreal
blue so intense as to bring tears. And in my mind the single
thought, that this was the way it was supposed to be.
    From my year in South Vietnam, I do not recall another
moment like that one, beautiful, poignant, peaceful, a little sad,
almost an epiphany. This song was an attempt to recapture a
moment that may have been once-in-a-lifetime.

1110 Bernie Fisher

Early in March in the year sixty-six
The men in the A Shau were in a bad fix
For three hundred friendlies the odds were all wrong
The enemy out there was two thousand strong

Air strikes might save them, but weather was bad
Still, we'd all give them the best that we had
With mountains on all sides and clouds everywhere
We just couldn't get enough airplanes in there

For two nights and two days the battle raged on
We knew in our hearts that they couldn't hold on
VC were pounding with mortar and gun
A Shau would be theirs before day was done

    Up from Pleiku came the trusty A -1
    Led by Bernie Fisher in HOBO Five - one
    He'd no way of knowing what his fate had planned
    Or the deed he would do before this day would end

The men in the camp said they needed help now
He knew that he had to get down there, but how
Then spotting a hole in the clouds down below
He strung out the flight and dove into the show

Out of the clouds roared the flight of A -1s
Straight down "the Tube," in the teeth of the guns
AKs and tracers were filling the air
Ten ways of dying were waiting down there

> Down on the airstrip an A -1 is down
> The pilot's alive, with VC all around
> "No time for a chopper," thought HOBO Five one
> It was then that he knew just what had to be done

With three other A -1s covering for him
He put down his wheels and then took it on in
Landed that Skyraider, turned it around
Then Myers came running 'cross that deadly ground

By the seat of his pants he was pulled in the plane
It was hard on his head, but he didn't complain
Out of the valley of death rode these two
Into the clouds and back home to Pleiku

> They asked Fisher why he went in there alone
> He said, "You don't leave him when he's one of your own."
> When men tell this story to men years from now
> They'll still speak of Glory that day at A Shau

Bernie Fisher   *Toby Hughes*
From *What The Captain Means: A Song of the In-Country Air War*
©2005   William F. "Toby" Hughes

On 10 March 1966 one of the most miraculous feats of rescue of modern warfare took place.

Flying in support of the besieged Special Forces camp in the A Shau valley of South Vietnam, Major Dafford "Jump" Myers was forced to land his battle damaged A-1E Skyraider on the camp's small airstrip, a runway at the time surrounded by the attacking enemy forces. That he survived the landing and the ground fire directed at him on arrival is a tribute to his own skill and good fortune, and is a miracle overshadowed only by the one that followed.

Major Bernard F. Fisher, overhead in another A-1, observed the crash landing below. Seeing the downed airman running from the burning plane, and realizing that time would run out for the man on the ground long before a rescue helicopter could arrive, Fisher elected to attempt the pickup himself. With his wingman and a second pair of A 1s covering, Major Fisher landed on the debris strewn airstrip, pulled Major Myers aboard his aircraft, and took off again, under constant fire from the enemy force all the while. When he landed at Pleiku he had nineteen bullet holes in his aircraft. Also in his aircraft was one unscheduled and grateful passenger who, because of Fisher's selfless heroism, would live to see another day.

For this action, Major Bernard Francis Fisher was awarded the Medal of Honor, the first of thirteen U. S. Air Force recipients in the Vietnam conflict of the nations's highest award for heroism.

There is only one line in this song about the assistance provided by "three other Skyraiders." Giving credit where it is due, these aircraft were flown by Captain Francisco Vasquez, Major Fisher's wingman, and Captains Jon Lucas and Dennis Hague, in the second flight. The part played by these men in this heroic drama is a matter of record, and it is to them, as well as to Majors Fisher and Myers, that this song is dedicated.

Douglas A-1E "Skyraider"
USAF Museum

1111 One-Level Gunner

There's a one-level gunner, out chained to a tree
Just off the runway he's waiting for me
The tracers come up in a dotted red line
But the bullets are always a little behind
I still sometimes wonder if one will be mine

> *The Yankee Air Pirates live right over there*
> *My job is to shoot when they take to the air*
> *To shoot down a Phantom would be a great deed*
> *But they're small and I can't seem to draw a good bead*
> *They're fast and I can't seem to pull enough lead*

That gunner's been out there for twenty-one days
Shooting in daylight and darkness and haze
He ain't hit nobody, and that's a bit strange
I'm afraid any day now that our luck will change
And that one-level gunner will soon find the range

> *Some might feel different, but I like it here*
> *Uncle Ho sends me nuoc mam and bullets and beer*
> *Don't live underground where it's clammy and damp*
> *Don't hide in a spider hole slimy and cramped*
> *I won't die on the wire of a Green Beret camp*

꒰) ☀ ☼ ◉

We can go out and get him anytime that we choose
Just blow him away with some good CBUs
But that would be cruel and stupid to boot
An unwise decision that bears bitter fruit
If the gomers replace him with one who can shoot

I'm a nine-level gunner, the best that we've got
I can hit what I aim at with only one shot
Can bring down a Phantom in a big blazing heap
But it's been well said, 'as ye sow shall ye reap'
And napalm for breakfast ain't my cup of tea

In my mind I can see him in his pointed hat
Cleaning his AK on a little straw mat
With fish cakes and rice and a Ba Muoi to drink
He smiles and he looks and he gives me a wink
And maybe he's smarter than some of us think

I'm happy with my way of fighting the war
Shoot ten feet behind as the Phantoms fly o'er
I don't bother them and they don't bother me
And I'll live here forever, chained to my own tree
In this nice little spot by the South China Sea

A Matter Of Mutual Respect *Toby Hughes*

From *What The Captain Means: A Song of the In-Country Air War*
©2005   William F. "Toby" Hughes

As in any other war, there were many undocumented tales, fables, rumors, and legends passed around among the participants. Some were true; some were false. Some were funny; some were sad. Some were long; some were short. Some were loud; some were quiet. Some were exciting; some were boring. *All* were worth a listen.

One of the more interesting and entertaining ones, apocryphal as it might be, was the one about the one-level VC gunner who resided off the end of the runway at Danang. Chained to a tree so that he could not desert his post, his mission was to shoot at the aircraft arriving and departing the air base. This he did, but to the wonder of all involved, he never hit anything. An evaluation of the situation by local security made the decision to leave him unmolested, as he was doing no harm, and if he were to be silenced, the enemy might replace him with a better gunner.

"One-level" refers to degree of skill on the job. In the old USAF specialty code, Level 1 was minimum entry-level proficiency at one's job tasks. The scale was graduated up to 9, indicating expert skill level. While our Charlie off the end of the runway was definitely performing at a one-level, one has to wonder if he was really that bad. Was he, as it seemed, just a bad shot in a job above his skills, or was he smarter than he was given credit for? Either way, it was a good story, and deserved a song.

Here is the story, as told from both sides.

Tuff enuff in the right hands

1112 Rolling Thunder

He's tried to put the war behind
But forgetting's not as easy as it seems
There's a demon lurking in his mind
At night it takes him back there in his dreams
      The clouds of flak,
      The MiGs' attack
      The vision of the missile's fiery plume
And he wakes sitting up in bed
With memories pounding in his head
And the sound of rolling thunder in the room

The whiskey helps to calm the fears
But there are still some ghosts that just won't die
Like the shimmer of the heat waves off the runway
As the strike force takes the sky
      The misty ridge
      The river bridge
      The rattle of the FAN SONG's deadly sound
And then the lightning fills the sky
And some will live and some will die
With crashing rolling thunder all around

To those who cannot understand
And those who, in their ignorance, criticize
Do not attempt to judge the man
Until you've seen the horror through his eyes

Of days in hell

Of friends who fell

Of vanished youth he nevermore will find

Of dreams that roll on endlessly

And memories that won't set him free

And waves of rolling thunder in his mind

Song For a Friend   *Toby Hughes*

From *What The Captain Means: A Song of the In-Country Air War*

©2005   William F. "Toby" Hughes

With thanks to Chip Dockery, for a moving and heartfelt rendition of the song.

In the classic western movie *The Outlaw Josey Wales,* the hero, in reflecting on his time in battle, says, "I guess we all died a little in that damn war."

Some died a lot.

Most of us who came home did so relatively intact. We put the war behind as much as was possible, and got on with our lives. We made our homes, loved our families, raised our children, proceeded down our various career roads, and although we never forgot our experience, we learned to live with the memories.

But not all of us. Some were scarred deeply by experiences that most of us will never know. I have known some of these men; one was a close and dear friend. He was intelligent, bright, witty and outgoing. He was a great guitar picker and a pretty good singer. He was an incredibly talented writer. He was one helluva fighter pilot. Once he was filled with the promise of youth, living his dream of flight, but the war brought his world crashing down around him. He lived out his last years raging against the demons within him, part of that group of veterans once described as "standing in front of the Wall, looking *through* the granite, hearing sounds the rest of us do not hear." But he never stopped raging, and the demons never broke his fighter pilot's spirit. When it was time for the final RTB, it came on his own terms.

Godspeed, old friend. May you find those skies where the weather is CAVU, the tanker is always on station, the RHAW gear is quiet, the wingmen are tucked in tight, and the flying is good again. Save me a slot on the schedule.

1113 Prowlin'

Runway Three Zero, takeoff roll
Listen to those afterburners roar!
Gear up, flaps up Two's moving in
Heading for the fight once more
   Well I've been a Phantom pilot here for months
   Wouldn't have it any other way
Than flying F-4's with the 13th Panther Pack
Prowlin' in the night and the day

Two called out "Lead, Break Hard Right!
You've got 37 tracking too close!"
Then he rolled in with Mark 82's
And put 'em right down that gunner's throat
   Well the trucks were stalled and we had a ball
   Blowing their shit away
Hey, ain't nothing better than flying with the Pack
Fighting in the night and the day

Vang Pao and his men were stuck on a ridge
Close to the PDJ
The North Viets had been giving him fits
For the better part of two or three days
   Well the weather was bad and the situation sad
   'Till a Raven put us back in the fray
Put the bombs on the smoke, man it ain't no joke
I love doing this all night and all day

Well the years have gone by and I still love to fly

It ain't bad at middle age

As a flyer or a lover, in the weeds or top cover

Still better'n most guys half my age

But there's times when the fire in the blood runs higher

I need a Phantom screaming into the wind

I'd give half I've got, for one more shot

To be flying with the Panthers again

Yeah, I'd give half I've got, for one more shot

To be flying with the Panthers again

. . . takes me back . . .   *Chip Dockery*

Every now and then something happens — maybe a call from an old buddy, for some reason I look at the old pictures, I play some of these songs, I go to an airshow — whatever, it takes me back. And I remember what Saburo Sakai, Japan's highest scoring ace to survive WWII, said in his book "Samurai!" . . . sometimes, many years later, when he closed his eyes he could still feel the throttle in his left hand, the stick in his right, the rudder bar under his feet, and could hear and feel his Zero's engine pulling him toward the sky. I know that feeling.

This song is an "old Fighter Pilot thinks back" song. The stuff in it really happened. As I recall, Capt John Sellers was the #2 who got the gun in Steel Tiger, and there were several times when the 13 TFS assisted the Raven FACS in saving General Vang Pao up in Barrel Roll.

1114 Holy Shit!

My Squadron CO, he said to me, 'You're gonna leave your F-4D
And go the fly where propellers swing
Learn how slow-movers do their thing.'

And so I went to NKP, their PE Sergeant, he howled with glee
"You ain't gonna need this", he said and laughed
And took away my oxygen mask

> These guys are crazy, they're all insane
> They fly their pre-historic planes
> From a jungle airfield, where the recips roar
> At NKP, on the Mekong's shore

The A-1 driver, he said to me, "Why try to hit, what you can't see."
So he rolled in from, four thousand feet
And pullled out damn near in the trees

> These guys are crazy, with balls of brass
> They'll use the prop to chop Commie ass
> They'll root around down among the trees
> Then fly on back to NKP

In an A-26, in the night time dark we found a convoy
Near an old truck park
We nailed the lead truck, and then bombed 'em all
Then strafed a gun site, with fifty cal

> Those guys are crazy, they have no fright
> They'll piss with the guns, in the dead of the night
> In an ancient warbird, built in '43
> Still fighting on, from NKP

With an O-2 FAC, call sign of "Nail"
We trolled along the Ho Chi Trail
Just a-dodging gunfire, and slinging Willy Pete
Way too damn low and slow for me

These guys are crazy, they have no fear
They live on AVGAS, cordite and beer
They'll fly 'em back, shot full of holes
To NKP, where the Mekong flows

Then I went back, to Udorn Thani, to my oxygen mask, and my F-4D
And to my CO, later that day gave my report, and to him did say

These guys are crazy, they've come unhinged
Their whole damn life's a flying fighting binge
And I'm damn glad that I got to see how the slow movers live, at NKP

... most indelible memory ...   *Chip Dockery*
This song relates one of the most memorable experiences
of my entire life. In October 1968, the 13 TFS commander sent
me over to Nakon Phanom RTAFB to fly with the "slow movers"
and get some idea of how their war and ours could be coordinated
better. When I checked in with their PE, the sergeant saw my
oxygen mask and literally said "What the hell is this from, the
Creature of the Black Lagoon?" and replaced it with a boom mic.

Across the next few days I flew day combat in the A-1
and 0-2, and night combat in the A-26 and C-123K. Later back
at Udorn I got night combat in the AC-47. It was all several
thousand feet lower and a few hundred knots slower than I was
used to, and totally 200% Shit Hot.

It's hard to say what was the most indelible memory, but
it was probably sitting behind Maj Grobe and his co-pilot in the
A-26 diving toward a gun site near some trucks we'd just
bombed, all 8 .50 cals in the nose lit up, cordite all over, and
every gun on that part of the Ho Chi Minh Trail shooting back.

A-1E Skyraider

Leader of our 2-ship on the way out

1115 Singha Hero

We were capping west of Hanoi on a somewhat cloudy day
When the SAM's launched, climbing skyward
Come to blow our shit away

CHORUS

Lord I don't want to be no hero
My Mom don't want no golden star
I just want a tall, cold Singhai
In the bar, Lord, in the bar

I was jinking off the target one dark night at old Tchepone
When a clip of 37 damn near blew my ass back home

CHORUS

I was Blue Four, on a BARCAP, the one the MiGs were coming for
When I got a fire light on my left engine
What a fucked-up way to go to war!

CHORUS

I was pressing on a target just a little south of Dong Hoi
When a ZPU stitched my airplane, blew holes all in my mach 2 toy

CHORUS (twice)

Singha Hero *Chip Dockery*

This is kind of a log book compilation song covering 1968 through 1972. Verse 1 (1972) is generic to Linebacker in the summer of 72. The SAMs mentioned were actually after one of our other flights some distance away and they all thankfully missed. Verse 2 (1968) recalls a clip of 37mm that basically had my AC, Maj R.O.Case, and I nailed as we pulled off the target. To this day, I think there was a God-given F-4 sized space between the third and fourth rounds in that clip.

The verse 3 (1972) story resulted in our 4 ship becoming a 3 ship + 1 crippled straggler (me) some miles prior to the merge. That was my "unhappiest for the longest" time ever. Fortunately for us, the MiGs found someone else to play with that day. The verse 4 (1969) action resulted in hits on the inboard pylons and on the tail, one of which blew away the drag chute. Maj Jim Bob Pascall was my AC for that one. After landing the brakes were a tad warm. Oh yeah, Singhai — the national beer of Thailand, damn good, I still love it.

. . . *and Dick Jonas chimes in with "Damn straight! It was spelled with the (umlauted — look it up in your WU) Kennedy 'a' on the end, but we all pronounced it with the 'ai' diphthong (look that one up, too) like in the picture caption below. Goo-o-d beer!"*

Singhai
Tall, cold, 1 ea

1116 Old O-2 Pilot's Tale

I'll sing you the story as he told it to me
'Twas back there, oh, some time ago
He was old and craggy, his flight suit was baggy
But his eyes had a wonderful glow
      He said, "The O-2 ain't fast, but, oh what the hell
      It's better than walking, I'd say
      You could bank, you could yank, and maybe get you a tank
      If the small arms didn't blow you away
They called it Skymaster; I'll tell you that bastard
Was never the world's greatest thrill
It's a two-motored bird, but let me give you the word
How one day I damn near got killed
      There's a "puller" in front and a "pusher" behind
      If one of them quits, things get rough
      If the back motor quits, it'll give you the fits
      'Cause the one up in front's not enough
I was marking some trucks, you know how that sucks
But the rockets were cooking off fine
Then both motors quit; God, I thought I was hit!
Below was rock, jungle, and pine
      I was too scared to fart, but I tried an airstart
      I knew I wouldn't make it in time
      But the back motor coughed and the damned thing lit off
      Or I wouldn't be here singing this rhyme
I gave the throttle a poke, hauled back on the yoke
I thought, "This just isn't my day."
My brain was on fire, I had the desire to yell, cuss out loud and to pray
I thought I would bash, but I didn't crash, I pulled out with nothing
      to spare

My voice was a squeak, my pants kinda leaked
"Hey! You fighters up there do your share!"
Flight lead came back with a wise-assed wisecrack
Saying, "You must be some kind of clown
Well, we've caught your act, but we gotta get back
So, FAC, quit your fucking around!"
The fighters rolled in, their bombs made a din
They made those damned trucks disappear
I gave BDA and I quit for the day, and went back to my base for a beer
If you've been up there and your front engine quit
It's something you've never forgot
You've been there, you've done that, and if you came home
You did it at just 80 knots
They called Skymaster — I called it other names
I've changed my mind and it's true
It's a great little bird and I give you my word my hat's off to the little O-2
Some said I was brave, I got a medal or two
I was lucky that I didn't crash
I feel so sublime when I think of that time
It's the O-2 that saved my old ass
(. . . repeat twice . . .)
. . . AND I'LL BET IT SAVED A LOT OF YOURS, TOO!

Old O-2 Pilot's Tale   *Irv LeVine*
     This one was easy to write; it is based on a *true* incident
that nearly took the life of the O-2 pilot. Carter "Chris" Neale related the incident to me as a mere happening and not the terrify-
ing event it must have been. Of course, it didn't happen exactly
as I wrote, but the fighter lead's words are exact. Heroes like
Chris are legion among Forward Air Controllers, but it is often
difficult to find them and make 'em admit to their deeds.
     I'm ever so proud to call Chris my friend. But he's more
than that; he represents the many just like him who were willing
to sacrifice it all for their fellowman and their country. Thanks,
Chris, and all you other guys who showed up when you were
needed most.

1117 My Iraqi Hacienda

In my Iraqi Hacienda (aha, ha, ha, haaaa), made of rocks & mud & sand
A foxhole here in Southwest Asia, courtesy of Uncle Sam
How I got here, isn't very clear, this is one crazy place
Up to my neck in muddy water (aha, ha, ha, ha, haaaa)
While dry sand's blowing in my face

In my Iraqi Hacienda, (aha, ha, ha, haaaa), there's a touch of Mexico
Spiders damned near big as wash tubs, and things that you don't
want to know
When setting sun says the long day is done
There's barely room in here for me
As evening mortar shells come callin' (aha, ha, ha, haaaa)
I'm joined by twenty-two or three

In my Iraqi Hacienda, (yee-e-en haaaa)
I cough, and cough, and cough and cough
It's HOT by day and cold by Noche
I melt then freeze my young ass off
While you are here, you can't get a beer
They say you must be PC all the way
Unless you get into the 'green zone' (wo-o, haaa)
And your ID reads CIA

In my Iraqi Hacienda, (wo-o, hoo, hoo, hoo, hoooo)
There's a lot of other grunts
They said, "You'll be here 90 days, boys,"
Tthen stretched that into 18 months

Hey! I'm not alone, we all want to go home
Back to the land of the big BX (yee-haw)
In my Iraqi Hacienda   (yee-e-e-ee Haw-w-w-w)
We're "screwed" but we don't think it's sex

In my Iraqi Hacienda, (aha, ha, ha, ha, haaaa), I don't feel I'm all alone
I'm here to try to help these people, but when the hell do I go home?
Hey, I'm a tough guy, I never, even cry
I'm not even sure that I feel fear
I've never been one for begging (aha, ha, ha, ha, haaaa)
But Lord, please get me outta here

Yeah! Get me outta here, man . . .
What's with this 'weekend warrior' shit? . . .
Where's that Freedom Plane everybody's talking 'bout, and why the
hell ain't I on it . . . Nobody gives a rats ass . . . but I sure do . . .
I'd be packed in 5 seconds . . .

. . . rocks & mud & sand . . .   *Irv LeVine*
    Like his father and grandfather before him he finds him-
self sitting in a foxhole he dug himself. Oh, they've changed the
name to 'sleeping hole' but it's still just a hole dug in dirt, dust
and sand. These materials have been around a lot longer than
his mere 17 to 22 years. He's not happy with this home away
from home but like all G.I.'s he makes the best of it and he does
it with humor and music. He hums, whistles, sings. Anything to
keep his spirits up — from sex-to-chow and back to sex.
    He combines what he knows may happen to what he
hopes will happen — which is going home and sex. He *knows* he's
going home. He's sure of it — but for now he has to "maintain
and innovate." His sleeping hole becomes his Hacienda. A place
of solitude and safety but with a humorous twist. His high
pitched notes are his way of shouting defiance at the world for
putting him in this place . . . and at the same time heralds his
joy at being alive. Everyone needs a Hacienda . . . if only in their
dreams.
    Ai-yi-yi-yiiiiiiiiiiiiiiiiii . . .

1118 Don't Bust Your Ass Fighter Pilot

I thought I'd like to fly for the Air Force
They'd keep me from harm every day
I soon learned from the start to dodge, duck, and fart
'Cause their mantra was "D.B.Y.A."
They taught me to fly, it was easy; to say things a pilot should say
I never got used to them shouting, "Hey, Kid, don't D.B.Y.A."

CHORUS

Don't bust your ass fighter pilot
Don't crash your plane all to hell
Don't bust your ass, it's so messy
Remember, you heard us all yell — D.B.Y.A.

I heard those words every morning, and often far into the night
I'd cover my ears, I tried humming, got so mad that I wanted to fight
A war came and soon they sent me, to fly, strafe, and bomb every day
One helluva pain, one helluva strain, when your brain says D.B.Y.A.

CHORUS

When the war was finally over, I got a job where I'd drive every day
What have I gained? Nothing has changed, my wife yells D.B.Y.A.
I've given you all fair warning
When you're fragged for a sortie some day
Don't bitch or crawl, do it balls to the wall, for godssake D.B.Y.A.

CHORUS

DBYA
Irv LeVine

If I heard D.B.Y.A. yelled in my direction once, I must have heard it a thousand times. Okay, so I'm exaggerating — a little. Maybe only 999. But, it's obviously stuck with me from pilot training through combat in the beautiful F-105 Thuderchief to my last days with the F-111 Aardvark.

No one wants to "bust" anything in the flying game, as the hack writers call military flying. So, D.B.Y.A. echoes in one's mind at the most inopportune times — like when the engine suddenly quits on a black-assed night, and things get real quiet, and you're over a huge mountain range, and . . . well, you get the picture.

But, whether you still fly or just find yourself driving to work on a daily basis, or maybe behind the wheel on a vacation trip, remember, you heard it here last . . . D.B.Y.A.!!!

F-111

To the best of my knowledge, the F-111 was born witihout a name. So, the guys who flew it named it *Aardvark.* Look at it for a minute and you'll see why. The Navy's F-14 Tomcat is it's fraternal twin, thanks to a guy named McNamara who didn't know shit about airplanes.

❀ ❦ ✣ ❦

1119 Tanker's Yodel

High up on a tank is where you'll find me
I came 'oer the ocean to set these folks free
It's a bit of a bitch but I've brought with me my very own tankers yodel
    This here's my Abrams, it's my house and my home
    I eat here, I sleep here and I'm not a lone
    There's 3 other guys and we all like to roam
    To the clank of this tank and my yodel
        YODEL

If it clanks it's a tank you can make a bet
If you hear it you're near it, it's the Army Corvette
There's no way to fight it when I'm here inside it
With it's gun and my tankers yodel
    I've heard some guys wondering "Why are we here?
    No booze and no women — not even a beer
    Just the sun and the sand and the weather so weird
    This tank and my tankers yodel."
        YODEL

I'm rolling along thinking "Why this all is."
They said in '91 "You're through with this biz."
The brass say's "It's swell." We just say, "Gee Whiz."
This tank & my tankers yodel
    We were all here back then, in Nineteen Ninety One
    We left too damned early before we were done
    On the dice roll this time you can bet on the come
    I'll yodel real soft 'til the shooting is done
        YODEL

The Cav *Irv LeVine*

    Some neat Cav guys challenged me to write some songs about tanks. Of course, I took the challenge. It was harder than I ever imagined. I read a lot of books on tanks, tank maneuverings, tanks made by other countries, improvements, and foul ups. I learned of the distinct bravery and sacrifice of the men who crew these leviathans of war.

    My concept was to keep it simple. I imagined someone whistling or humming while sorting out the complexities of his assignment and his equipment and the enemy's chances of being tougher than he was.

    My tanker yodeled his way throuh the night, the nightmares of the job, and the task he was more than willing to underatake in the name of freedom.

Abrams Tank

12

Digger, Loco, Bull, Dixie, JayBird, Tex, Taz, Skin

Juvat Boys Choir

Missing from picture: Elvis, Meat, Shadow, Nogas

Chrissy "Duke" Deibel

Becky "Coyote" Muggli

Carrie "HARB" Reinhardt

Kat "BD" Burkhead

Bonnie "Sassy" Pucillo

Fresh Out of the Box & Dick

Dos Gringos

Chris "Snooze" Kurek

Rob "Trip" Raymond

EROSONIC

" . . . The planes we flew . . . "

Juvat Boys Choir
T-3, T-41, T/A-37, T/AT-38, T-33,
T-39, A-4, O-2, OV-10
F/RF-4: 125 missions Vietnam
A-7: 51 missions Vietnam
F-100: 264 missions Vietnam
F-111 75 missions Vietnam
F-16: 144 missions
          Iraq/Bosnia/Serbia
      4 missions Noble Eagle
KC-135: 52 missions Vietnam

Fresh Out of the Box
T-3, T-37, T/AT-38
B-52: 21 missions Afghanistan
A-10: 146 missions
          Afghanistan/Iraq
F-16: 41 missions Iraq
      16 missions Noble Eagle

Dos Gringos
T-3, T-41, T-37, T/AT-38
F-16: 77 missions Iraq,
      20 missions Noble Eagle

1201 Passing the Flame

The time has come, the Master said, for the passing of the flame
The yielding of the torch, to those who've earned the fame
You've toiled in the skies above against the vaunted foe
Now you must leave the center stage; you've elsewhere to go

The flame was lit a century past, one hundred years gone by
It came to life at Kitty Hawk, where humans learned to fly
It burned its brightest in the deeds of warriors, brave and true
In battles fought beyond the clouds, in tales of derring-do

Mannock, Fonck, and Rickenbacker fanned the flame so high
And blazed a trail in blood and courage across a war-torn sky
The flame they passed to eager hands would burn yet brighter still
And light the names of heroes bold who dared to force their will

McCampbell, Foss, and Bong took up the flame and carried on
The fight against the foe which ended up the victory won
Others burned the flame as battles came and went
McConnell, Ritchie, Cunningham, all knew what courage meant

Now's the moment in your hand the flame burns clear and true
Handed down from men who looked and saw the good in you
You battled hard, you gave your all; you kept freedom free
So, hand off the fight to younger blood and go with dignity

} ∮ {

You're not the first, and neither last to watch your sun go down

Those who take your place today will see their time come 'round

So it goes, from hand to hand, to head, to heart, and eye

Forevermore the flame shall burn, so long as there's a sky.

... the flame ...   *Dick Jonas*

I got life figured out. If Satan walked up and said, "Give me your soul and you can have anything you want," and I was dumb enough to do that, I'd choose to be a . . .

. . . thirty-one year old captain, in the zone for major, sweating the next promotion list, flying a state-of-the-art hot fighter plane . . .

Young. Intelligent. Skilled. Responses an equal match for the epoxy and electrons and jet fuel and cordite.

It never quits. It never winds down. When the sun goes down, the ramp lights up like the Super Bowl. When the jocks shut the last one down and head for the Club, the crew chiefs tug 'em down to the run-up pad and torch 'em off again.

And the engines run all night tonight, to make sure they'll run all day tomorrow . . .

There's always tomorrow. Always.

. . . A thirty-one-year-old captain, sweating major, and flying the Stealth or the Eagle or the Viper or the Warthog or the Raptor . . . you're exactly in the heart of the envelope — D G Z.

(ref Eccl 93080507)

Point of the Spear

1202 I've Been Everywhere

Well, I took off from Ubon in a thick and heavy driving rain
I toted my bombs out to Green Anchor Tanker Plane
I had this brand new AC riding in the front seat
A guy with six months RTU, before that a 'Tweet'
He asked me if my counters numbered much more than ten
I said, "Listen, Mac, there ain't no place up there I ain't been."

CHORUS

I've been everywhere, Man, I've been everywhere
I crossed the mountains bare, Man, I seen the flak-filled air
Of SAMs I've had my share, Man, I've been everywhere

I been to Hanoi, Haiphong, Phuc Yen, Yen Bai
Lang Son, Hoa Lac, Phu Tho, Son Tay
Hoa Binh, Nam Dinh, Thai Binh, Bac Ninh
Thai Nguyen, Gia Lam, Viet Tri, Do Son
Thud Ridge, MiG Ridge, Northeast Railroad
Bac Mai, Ninh Giang, Bac Giang, Poo-yeng
CHORUS

I been to Sam Neua, Ban Ban, Quang Tri, Son La
Bat Lake, Dong Hoi, Quang Khe, Thanh Hoa
Red Route, Black Route, Blue Route, Purple Route
Channel 97 and the Red and Black River Valley
Land side, water side, down the slide, dang my hide
In town, cross town, up town, down town
CHORUS

I been to Taegu, Kwangju, Fuchu, Kunsan

Inchon, Osan, Pusan, Suwon

P-Y Do, Cheju do, Guam, Okinawa

Hachinohe, Morioka, Sendai, Wakkanai

Tachikawa, Itazuke, Niigata, Pohang

Kagoshima, Hiroshima, Ie Shima, hot dang!

CHORUS

I been to Seoul, Kimpo, Honolulu, Wake, Midway

Hong Kong, Bangkok, Baguio, Manila Bay

Hualien, Tainan, Taitung, Keelung

Chiayi, Hsin chu, Kaohsiung, Ping Tung

Saigon, Singapore, Tokyo, Taipei

Taichung city, all night, all day

CHORUS

Geography Lesson   *Dick Jonas*

If you'll procure yourself maps of Southeast Asia, Northeast Asia, and Southwest Asia, you should have no trouble staying oriented throughout this song.

All of a sudden it strikes me that the United States keeps going to war in Asia. Half of WWII was Asia and the Pacific. Oh, I know, there were Panama and Grenada, but our really big scraps seem to take place in Asia. Korea. Vietnam. Desert Storm. Afghanistan. Iraq.

Until 11 September 2001. *911.*

Chip, Chris, and I wrote our versions of "I've Been Everywhere" because we'd had some poignant experiences in the places we wrote about. Bullets; adrenalin — that kind of stuff.

The song with U. S. place names was written by an Australian by the name of Geoff Mack, and recorded by Hank Snow, Johnny Cash, and a bunch of other Americans. Getting shot at had nothing to do with that version.

If the war against terrorism goes well, there won't be any more home court battles to write about.

Air combat. It's extremely educational — in geography, if nothing else.

I've been everywhere man, I've been everywhere
I've bombed the mountains bare man, I've breathed the dust-filled air
Of flak I've had my share, man, I've been everywhere

Like Barrell Roll, Steel Tiger, Tally Ho, Tiger Hound
Barry's Bridge, Rat Fink, Nape Pass, Cricket West
Brown's Lake, Butterfly, Dong Hoi, Route South
Duck's Head, Dog's Head, Roadrunner, Fish's Mouth
Black Route, Red Route, Green Route, Quang Khe
And WAY down south where I wasn't supposed to be

Well I've worked with everybody man, all over this war-torn land
Guided by the radar's hand to dump bombs on a pile of sand
I've been FAC'd up, I've been FAC'd down
I've been FAC'd at every turn

By Invert. Bromo, Teepee, Dressy Lady
Hillsboro, Moonbeam, Sycamore, Ally Cat
Nail FAC, Covey FAC, Blind Bat, Raven FAC
Zorro FAC, Snort FAC, Candlestick, Stormy FAC
Wolf FAC, Firefly, Lamplighter, Misty FAC,
And now Falcon FAC from the big Panther Pack

Well I've done evereything man, I've done everything
Any mission you can name, man, I've flown it in a Fighter plane
I've put old Snoopy to shame man, I've done everything

Like Day Strike, Night Strike, Interdiction, Truck Kill
Road Rip, Storage Area, Close Support, Tree Park
Sky Spot, Nail Run, Mig Cap, Armed Recce,

Low Level, High Drag, Dive Bomb, Wing Gaggle
Gun Run, Two-Ship, Four-Ship, NIght Owl
Day Patrol, Night Patrol, Dawn Patrol, Onion Patrol

I've been everywhere, man, I've been everywhere
I've bombed the mountains bare, man, I've breathed the dust filled air
Of flack I've had my share, man, I've been everywhere

CHORUS

I've been to Basrah, Baghdad, Najaf, Samawah
Diwaniyah, Karbala, Tikrit, Fallujah
Key West, Kirkuk, H3, Mosul
Talil, Balad SE, Kandahar, Kabul
Al Taqaddum, Al Asad, Bagram, Jalalabad
No sod, lotta FOD, and I thought it kinda odd

CHORUS

I've been to Al Jaber, Al Udeid, Doha, Al Salem
PSAB, Thumrait, drank a beer in Bahrain
Osan, Kunsan, Diverted into Suwon
Grozni, Bosnia, Sarajevo, Kosovo
Uzbekistan, Tajikistan, Kyrgyzstan, Pakistan
And every other Stan that would let us bomb Afghanistan

CHORUS

1203 Lakes of Tally Ho

Fingers, Pork Chop, Butterfly, Bat, T-Bone
Waters of fire that the devil has claimed for his own
The fish don't bite and the boats don't row
And the gunners are out whenever you go
To Fingers, Pork Chop, Butterfly, Bat, T-Bone

Fingers, T-Bone, Butterfly, Bat, Pork Chop
They got quad-23's and the music don't never stop
The FIRECAN chirps and the triple-A zings
Every now and then the FAN SONG sings
At Fingers, T-Bone, Butterfly, Bat, Pork Chop

Fingers, Pork Chop, T-Bone, Bat, Butterfly
The man on the ground's full of hate for the man in the sky
He lives in the trees and he sleeps in the muck
He'll hang it all out for a hundred-dollar truck
At Fingers, Pork Chop, T-Bone, Bat, Butterfly

Fingers, Pork Chop, T-Bone, Butterfly, Bat
When you take it on down, heads up! Hold on to your hat!
Lookin' for the trucks and findin' the guns
Flyin' through the lead storm, ain't this fun?
At Fingers, Pork Chop, T-Bone, Butterfly, Bat

Pork Chop, T-Bone, Butterfly, Bat and Fingers
Precious memory, how it lingers
Five mileposts on the road to hell
All your life you'll remember them well
Pork Chop, T-Bone, Butterfly, Bat and Fingers

Fingers, Pork Chop, Butterfly, Bat, T-Bone
When the war's all over I'm coming back here all alone
Make one more pass and I know I won't miss
I'll stand on the banks and take a good piss
In Fingers, Pork Chop, Butterfly, Bat, T-Bone

Hate-filled, hair-trigger, hypertense hide-and-seek zone
Where two go in and one often comes out alone
And I pray for the day that the bastards are dry as a bone
Gimme five KT and I'll turn that mud to stone
Fingers, Pork Chop, Butterfly, Bat, T-Bone

The Lakes   *Toby Hughes*
From *What The Captain Means: A Song of the In-Country Air War*
©2005   William F. "Toby" Hughes

The air war in Vietnam was fought over land, but some of
the most vivid memories of that war are forever tied to bodies of
water. For those who flew in the "way up North war", two of
these will always hold a place in memory, the Gulf of Tonkin and
the Red River. For those who skirmished exclusively in the down-
south fray, the South China Sea and the Mekong River still echo
through the canyons of old men's memories. For those of us who
met in the middle and had the opportunity to enjoy (?) both sides
of the coin, there were some other little bodies of water that
somehow just won't go away.

Five little lakes, not much more than ponds, in the lower
part of Route Pack One, were landmarks for aircrews pulling that
delightful duty known as armed reconnaissance. The lakes were
easy to spot, easy to identify, as each conformed to a distinctive
geometrical pattern on the ground. Each bore a familiar shape,
and being the descriptive genii that we were, we were quick to
give them appropriate names.

When you crossed the DMZ, northbound at the mid-point,
you found yourself over a central lake with five dangling estuar-
ies. The visual pattern was that of a bony hand, the fingers dangling. We called the lake Fingers. Turn east toward the beach,
then head north up the highway, and you crossed over two more
little lakes, one resembling a pork chop, the other the centerpiece
of a prime cut of beef. We called those Pork Chop and T-Bone,
two choice cuts that sometimes eat *you*. Farther up the beach,
about five miles south of the Mi Le ferry, was the largest of the
lakes, shaped like a huge fluttering butterfly. Guess what we
called it. Passing over Butterfly, you checked out the ferry and
turned west, then back toward the southwest corner of the DMZ,
and halfway there you saw the thing that nightmares are made
of. Nestled in the foothills, just where the terrain begins its constant rise toward the Laotian border, painted on the barren
moonscape in the hues of its slate-gray water, lay an enormous
creature of the night.

Bat Lake was a horror. On clear and sunny days it rolled
in mists and malevolent fog. It was surrounded by guns and
burned and broken aircraft parts. More than a body of water, Bat
Lake was corporeal, and as much the enemy as the men who de-
fended it and called it home. The lake, on its own, seemed to
spawn trucks and supplies and guns. Bat Lake and Death were
old acquaintances.

Late one afternoon, with the falling sun hanging over the hills to the west, and Rich and I hanging inverted over Bat, pulling the nose down at the top of the pop-up, that damnable shape filling the windscreen, my flight suit a lot wetter than the inside of my mouth, I made a promise as to what I was going to someday return to this God-forsaken land and do. I haven't done it yet, but the desire is still there and always will be.

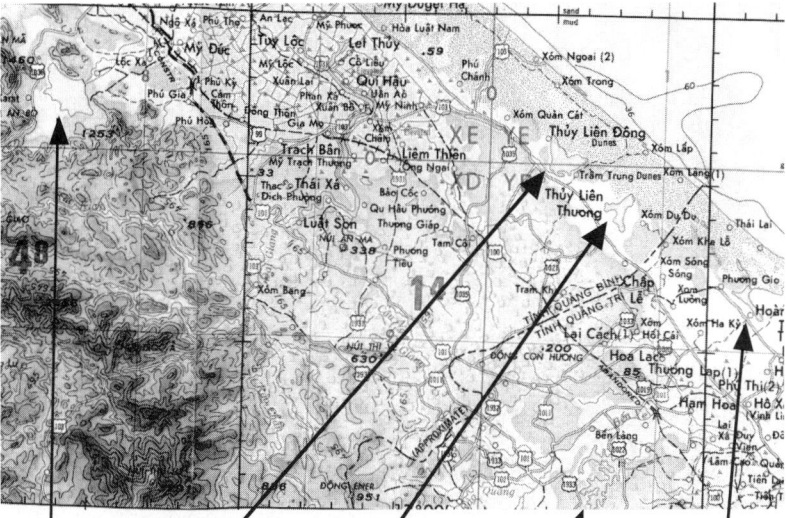

Bat   Butterfly   T-Bone   Fingers   Porkchop

12-8.2

1204 Call Out the Goddam Reserves

CHORUS

Call out, call out, call out the goddam Reserves (Reserves)
Call out, call out, call out the goddam Reserves

In peacetime the Regulars are happy
In peacetime they're anxious to serve
But just let them get into trouble; they call out the goddam Reserves

CHORUS

Oh, here's to the Regular Air Force, they have such a wonderful plan
They call out the goddam reservists whenever the shit hits the fan

CHORUS

They call out the war-weary pilots
They ask for the drafted young men
They send the Reserves to Korea, the Regulars stay in Japan

CHORUS

In peacetime the Regulars are happy,
They fill up the Pentagon's halls
From there they deploy the reservists
Whenever some new trouble calls

CHORUS

Flying high over the desert, the Regulars had all the fun
But now that the Gulf War is over
It's the Re-serves that sweat in the sun

CHORUS

So here's to the Regular Air Force
With their medals and badges galore
It it weren't for the goddam reservists
Their arse would be dragging the floor

CHORUS

1205 ZPU Gunner

CHORUS

A ZPU Gunner, a ZPU Gunner, a ZPU Gunner am I
A ZPU Gunner, a ZPU Gunner
If they give me a SAM site I'll die

I graduated at the top of my gunner's class
I worked hard, you will agree
But three classes behind, those guys that were blind
Got the same assignment as me

CHORUS

I asked for a Barrell Roll assignment
I said, "A Shit-Hot young gunner I am"
They gave me a block, on top of "The Rock"
Dodging CBU's and Panther Pack GAM's

CHORUS

So I asked for a Steel Tiger assignment
I got there one bright sunny day
That night by flare light, they laid 'em in tight
I wound up on O'Rourke's BDA

CHORUS

Well soon I crawled out of my spider hole, I put a new clip on my gun
The very next day, despite BDA
I hosed down Falcon One-One

CHORUS

Well I went PCS to Mu Ghia, to a two-seater 37 upgrade
But one thing I can't hack, it's that guy in the back
Telling me every mistake that I've made
He reads me all of the checklist, we pre-fire the gun in the pit
But if I shoot a bit low or am just a tad slow
The first thing I hear is "I've Got It!!"

CHORUS

We read the Yankee frag daily, we know who's flying, who's not
We sit in the shade, while the passes are made, reading sex
magazines, smoking pot

CHORUS

Dick: Just for the record . . .   *Chip Dockery*
    In verse 2, the original lyrics were "dodging CBU's and
Hestel's GAM's" This was a reference to Hestel D. Estes, one of
the more notorious members of the Pack. Sometime when we're
having a couple of tall cool ones and tellin' yarns, remind me to
tell you some Hestel stories.
    I found out when singing the song for various audiences
that so many explanations were required already that I dropped
all personal references for the sake of the overall performance.
The same for Verse 3 which mentioned "O'Rourke's BDA". I really
wish I had used both their names for your "posterity" recording,
but at the time habit got the upper hand. If you can work in
some version of this note giving both guys credit I'd appreciate it.

Gunner   *Chip Dockery*

Back in 1969, I was a GIB (F-4 backseater, Guy In Back) half-way through my first combat tour. At that time, every USAF GIB was a guy who had graduated high enough in UPT to get fighters, but not high enough to get a single-seater, assuming there were any available for that class. There was no such thing as a first assignment to an F-4 front seat. That came later.

Although life as a GIB in the 13th TFS "Panther Pack" at Udorn RTAFB was pretty darn good, we still wanted our own gunsight. During a couple of days off, a severe "Scotch front" moved through the hootch and we were commiserating about our GIB-hood and life in general, and somehow the subject got raised if the guys on the "other side" had to put up with stuff like that. I got to thinking that most probably they did in one form or another. At that time the war had no MiGs in it, so I focussed on the guys we most often fought every day . . . the gunners and the truck drivers. For this song, I wrote what hopefully was a humorus take on the fact that no matter what military you're in, you will get a ration of similar crap somewhere along the line . . . in this case, the process of selection into equipment, having to work as a crew, and experiencing both ends of ordnance delivery. Dick Jonas' excellent song *Yankee Air Pirate* provided the tune and lyric format.

Never took a pic of a ZPU, but here is a 37 MM
'liberated' in Laos and brought to Udorn.

Special thanks to Chip Dockery for the photos on this page.

"Two's in!"

A-26 Nimrod

" . . . a mighty hunter before the Lord . . . "

Night mission

Check the inboards and centerline. This guy means business!

1206   Doumer Bridge

18 December '67, at noon like a thunder clap
We dropped Doumer Bridge on down into Ho Chi Mins wet lap
      CHORUS
Well now boys . . .
      We fought the battle of Doumer Bridge
      Doumer Bridge, Doumer Bridge
      We fought the battle of Doumer Bridge
      And the bridge went tumbling down

Now you talk about your River Kwai Bridge
And the one at Thanh Hoa, too
We dropped seven spans of the Doumer Bridge
Down into the mud and goo
      CHORUS

Ho says he plays all the cards boys, and he does so with great joy
I wonder how he liked our game of 'bridge' up at old Hanoi
      CHORUS

Now we left some friends up yonder due to SAMS and MiGs and flak
And if Ho puts that damned bridge up well we'll all be goin' back
      CHORUS

For those who've gone before us, for those on that far shore
I know we'll not forget them soon, let's sing it just once more

      CHORUS (twice)

The Battle Of Doumer Bridge   *Irv LeVine*

The first partially successful raid on the Doumer Bridge was by done by the "tigers" from Tahkli. The renowned John Piowaty was given credit for knocking down *one* (and it was *only one*) of the Doumer Bridge supports on that one.

18 December '67, the 388th Wing was fragged for the next try. As the song points out, "We knocked seven spans of the Doumer Bridge down into the mud and goo." A hurried pontoon bridge was built across the river by the North Vietnamese and we pounded it too. A terrible carnage by the two determined forces . . . only we didn't have to chain our people to our aircraft as they had to for their guns.

A bit one sided you say? Better ask the guys that flew against those guns and were welcomed at the Hanoi Hilton by their captors after they were shot down.

1207   Cav Tanker's Boogie

Hannibal's animal, the elephant, was history's very first tank
The beast was big but it handled the gig
It squealed but it never did clank
Then nothing was done until World War One
When a monster rolled out of the gloom
It traveled on treads and caused so much dread
The Jerries all thought they were doomed

> CHORUS
> Oh the clank of a tank is an ominous sound
> It will fill your young heart full of dread
> Don't mess with a tank or the guys inside it
> Or you just may wind up dead

If it "clanks" it's a tank, believe it
There's no other sound like that sound
Don't piss it off or mistreat it, It'll grind your young ass in the ground
Years quickly passed, they refined it,
"It's bigger and better," they said
But no matter the make or the model it still ran around on a tread
> CHORUS

It's silouette's low and it's mobile, it's fast and can turn on a dime
It's full of boards and computers, hell, it might even get you "on line"
Be careful what you say about it , a tanker may be close bye
If he doesn't like what you just called it you just may get a black eye
> CHORUS

Progress is progression they tell us, a "Land Ship" from the War One
They've added a lot of gadgets since then, including all kinds of guns
It's made of steel and composites you know they're tougher than Hell
It's loaded with all kinds of weapons
With cannon, machine guns, and shells
CHORUS

They're big and they're fast and they're comin'
You'll know you're in deep shit
If they see you they'll kill you for certain
And my friend that hurts quite a bit
You may have heard it before, friend
But they'll gladly remind you of it
You may be "shithot" where you come from
BUT IF YOU AIN'T CAV YOU AIN'T SHIT!!
CHORUS
That's D-E-A-D dead . . . Tits UP . . . Kaput . . . Mortè!
Fini Walloo . . . gone . . .

. . . and break things . . .   *Irv LeVine*
AGAIN! "Why don't nobody write any songs about
tanks?" Well, AGAIN! "I really don't know." They're big, bad,
and comin', and nobody in his right mind wants to really mess
with a tank. They have a helluva history in combat, both good
and bad. The world loves tanks, so why don't more songs get
written about 'em?
RESEARCH!
I've talked to tankers and they're a pretty close-mouthed
bunch, unless they've been drinking. Even then you don't get the
feel of their lives as easily as you do, say, an Air Force pilot or a
Naval aviator. A tank is a direct, at you, killing machine. Their
crews think a lot of their tank and themselves. Only
natural. Their job is to *attack* or *defend*, and in the process of doing either they tend to kill people and break things. Their motto,
IF YOU AIN'T CAV YOU AIN'T SHIT, stems from the very
heart of the monster they push, prod and drive into battle. You
can assume the word 'shit' in this case has a positive meaning.

1208 The Choir

Away out here we got a gang
That sets their hair on fire
With Juvat tea and pressure bar
The boys they call the choir
      The choir, the choir, they call us the boy's choir

Songs of filth and perversion
And women we desire
If you don't want to hear those songs
Fuck off! we're not for hire
      The choir, the choir, they call us the boy's choir

Singing songs of tits and ass
And pissin' off the pounders
We don't care who we gross out
It's JayBird who gets fired
      The choir, the choir, they call us the boy's choir

Stuck out here so near the edge
We put our bombs on target
We fly our jet as we know how
And the Falcon she's our harlot
      The choir, the choir, they call us the boy's choir
          The choir, the choir; fuck off! We're not for hire

(⚷ ⚶)

. . . not for hire . . .   *Sean "Hyde" Renbarger, JBC Lead 2005*
    The Choir is the opening song sung by one of the most elite and least respected groups in the world — the Juvat Boys Choir. They started out as a joke in 1973, but turned into one of the last bastions of fighter pilot history and tradition. Their goals remain the same — drink, party, bullshit, and sing the tales of fighter pilots past and present. Heroics and buffoonery — and of course, make fun of pounders and Tooeys.
    Fuck off! We're not for hire!

JBC Patch

Worn proudly by at least one Juvat song warrior.

1209 Mamas Don't Let Your Babies Grow Up To Be Juvats

CHORUS
Mama's don't let your babies grow up to be Juvats
Don't let 'em shoot missiles and roll in on trucks
Let 'em be doctors and make lots of bucks
Mama's don't let your babies grow up to be Juvats
They'll never stay sober, they're always hungover
Even on old JayBird's wing

Juvats ain't easy to love and they're hard to control
They'd like to frag MPC for all the bullshit they're sold
Gas masks and flak vests and little tin helmets and sirens that drive
      them insane
If you don't understand 'em and most colonels don't
You'd think that they've burned out their brains
      CHORUS

Juvats love OB and soju and small-titted yobos
Little kun-dingies and nurses and anything in sight
Them that don't know 'em won't like 'em and them that do
      sometime won't know how to take 'em
They ain't wrong, they're just different and their pride won't
Let 'em forget that the Juvats are best!
      CHORUS

. . . hard to control . . .   *Dick Jonas*

An astute observer once noted that if today's fighter pilots had lived a century or two ago, we would all have been cowboys. No pickup trucks, of course, but I'm sure we would have been quite handy with a six-gun.

By the same token, if John Wesley Hardin, the James boys, the Daltons, Billy the Kid, et al were to suddenly transplant to the 21st century, you'd have the best luck finding them on a fighter flight line.

It's no wonder that this generation's 'warrior bards' have appropriated the tunes from so many cowboy songs in which to clothe our doggerel. See, what we go for first is image. It's got to roll smoothly off the tongue. It's got to sound cool. It's got to have impact. Cowboy songs do that better than any other genre.

Today's fighter pilot is just a cowboy with a titanium horse and a six-barrelled Gatling gun with much bigger bullets and a phenomenal rate of fire. (I'm sure 100 bullets per second qualifies as phenomenal.)

Baby Juvat
Lovable little critters, aren't they?

1210 Goin' In For Guns

I was on my ACT upgrade standard 4 v X
The AWACs guy was out to lunch so I couldn't get no decs
I knew that they were hostile but I couldn't take the chance
So flipped the switch to outboard and said "boys it's time to dance"

And he asked me where ya going as I started to diverge
Said I've had enough of this shit, man, I'm going to the merge
'Cause BVR is great, but it's time to have some fun
So Darkstar 'Judy Judy,' I'm going in for guns

I was flying as a bandit doing dark grey WIC support
I was out there by my lonesome 'cause my buddy was a mort
I saw that big fat fucker in a turn off to my right
He was either lost or he was looking for a fight

So I put him in my HUD and I almost flipped the switch
But then I thought how could I miss 'cause that's a huge bitch
And only a big pussy would use his 2 fox ones
It's time to get medieval; I'm going in for guns

We were back in Iraq for the 2nd set
Killing every fucking thing that they parked in a revet
When I saw me close to 69 trucks parked in a row
And I knew I shouldn't do it but I just could not say no

❀ ✳ ⚘ 🌿 ♔ ⚘ ⚘ 🌿 ♔ ⚘

And I called up 20 mike-mike and I rolled in for the pass
Knowing my commander he was gonna chew my ass
This issue's black and white like a school bus full of nuns
Someone's gotta make the call, I'm going in for guns

I'd gone out for Mexican; my stomach was in knots
From a greasy chimichanga and 2 tequila shots
We had to step in 5 for my one DACT
As I yelled over my shoulder "Don't nobody wait for me!"

And I'm running down the hall like I'd never run before
And I began to wonder if I'd make it to the door
'Cause every second counts when you're ass has got the runs
And I made the call behind the stall, "I'm going in for guns!"

Guns   *Chris "Snooze" Kurek*
    A little humor mixed in with some true stories. The first
two verses merely express what every fighter pilot feels. That is,
a kill is nice. But a "guns track" kill is truly something to behold.
The last 2 verses are based on true stories. No, it didn't happen
to me. Those who it did happen to know who they are. But I ain't
tellin'.

1211 TDY Again

TDY again
Just can't wait to go TDY again
The life I love is out at Nellis with my friends
And I can't wait to go TDY again

TDY again
Just can't wait to go TDY again
Out at Binion's where the party never ends
And I can't wait to go TDY again

    TDY again
    Leaving all the queep and bullshit far behind you
    In trouble again, knowing that your better half can't find you
    Or she won't mind you . . . being

TDY again
Just can't wait to go TDY again
The life I love is getting stupid with my friends
And I can't wait to go TDY again

    TDY again
    Going double down and splitting up my aces
    " ?? Two ?? Ah, SHIT!! "
    ATM again, throwing up in all the nicest places
    You should see our faces

When we go home again
It's gonna hurt when we go home again
She'll shove that credit card bill right up my rear end
It's gonna hurt when we go home again
And I swear I'll never go TDY again
Yeah, I swear I'll never drink that much again
Yeah, I swear I'll never gamble again
That is until I go TDY again . . .

TDY   *Chris "Snooze" Kurek*

Going to Vegas with a fighter squadron. 'Nough said.

1212 Sammy Small

Oh, my name is Sammy Small, fuck 'em all
Oh, my name is Sammy Small, fuck 'em all
Oh, my name is Sammy Small, and I've only got one ball
But, it's better than none at all, so fuck 'em all

Oh, they say I shot a man, fuck 'em all
Oh, they say I shot a man, fuck 'em all
Oh, they say I shot 'im dead, with a piece of fuckin' lead
Now that silly fucker's dead so fuck 'em all

Oh, they say I'm gonna swing, fuck 'em all
Oh, they say I'm gonna swing, fuck 'em all
Oh, they say I'm gonna swing from a piece of fuckin' string
What a silly fuckin' thing, so fuck 'em all

Oh, they say I greased the rope, fuck 'em all
Oh, they say I greased the rope, fuck 'em all
Oh, they say I greased the rope, with a piece of fuckin' soap
What a silly fuckin' joke, so fuck 'em all

Oh, the parson he will come, fuck 'em all
Oh, the parson he will come, fuck 'em all
Oh, the parson he will come, with his tales of kingdom come
He can shove it up his bum, so fuck 'em all

Oh, the sheriff will be there, too, fuck 'em all
Oh, the sheriff will be there, too, fuck 'em all
Oh, the sheriff will be there, too, with his silly fuckin' crew
They've got fuck-all else to do, so fuck 'em all

Oh, the hangman wears a mask, fuck 'em all
Oh, the hangman wears a mask, fuck 'em all
Oh, the hangman wears a mask, for his silly fuckin' task
He can shove it up his ass, so fuck 'em all

I saw Molly in the crowd, fuck 'em all
I saw Molly in the crowd, fuck 'em all
I saw Molly in the crowd, and I felt so fuckin' proud
That I shouted right out loud, so fuck 'em all

Sammy   *Chris "Snooze" Kurek*
This one is always a crowd favorite. Most of our songs
don't lend themselves to "rockin' out," and that's tough for two
guys who grew up on rock. So we just updated an old classic to
allow ourselves to live out our rock star fantasies.

1 2 1 3 I Wish I Had a Gun Just Like the A-10

Oh, I wish I had a gun just like the A-10
I'd be happy as a baby in a playpen
I'd mow 'em down like a weed eater
With that thirty millimeter
I wish I had a gun just like the A-10
  Oh, I wish I had eight AMRAAMS like the Eagle
  I'd be having so much fun it'd be illegal
  Like a guy who aint been laid for months
  I'd shoot those fuckers all at once
  I wish I had eight AMRAAMS like the Eagle
Oh, I wish I had the gas just like a Mudhen
To hang around that long is just a sin
While you RTB and scoff
I'm doing loops and jackin' off
I wish I had the gas just like a Mudhen
  Oh, I wish I had the alpha of a Hornet
  Living to fight slow when others scorn it
  When I can still pitch and roll
  That other guy's going outta control
  I wish I had the alpha of a Hornet
All you fuckers wish you flew the Viper
Probably since the time you wore a diaper
We got every mission that you do
And we fly 'em all better than you
Yeah all you fuckers wish you flew the Viper

    𝄞 ⚜ ⚜ ⚜

'Cause we're single seat multi-role

We can fly right up our own asshole

Yeah, all you fuckers wish you flew the Viper

. . . I wish . . .   *Chris "Snooze" Kurek*

Those who don't fly the Viper always say that it is the jack of all trades and the master of nothing. Never did I hear this more than when I became an IFF instructor. There is some truth to that idea, I guess. It would always be nicer to have more weapons, more gas, more nose authority and so on.

But I'd never trade a day flying the Viper for anything else. Anyway, I wrote this song to have a little fun with my friends who don't enjoy the privilege of flying the Viper. Hey, we're all on the same team, right?

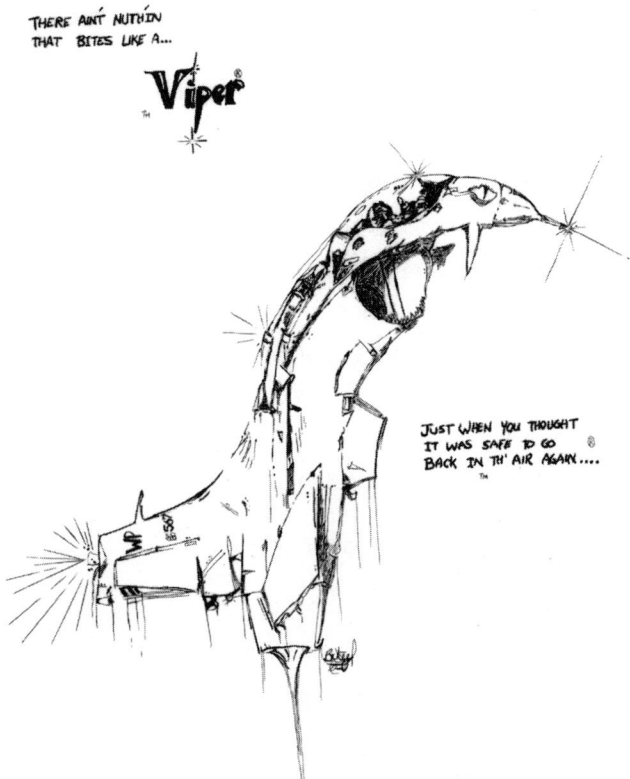

THERE AIN'T NUTHIN THAT BITES LIKE A...

Viper

JUST WHEN YOU THOUGHT IT WAS SAFE TO GO BACK IN TH' AIR AGAIN....

1214 Bingo Over Baghdad

I launched outta Jaber at a quarter to 2
Four by slammer and GBU
Hit the tanker and headed on into the fight
I started looking up and down the road
And then I found myself the motherload
And I knew I was going to clean my rails that night

> CHORUS
> Now I'm bingo over Baghdad I used all the gas that I had
> Bombing every BMP from there to Basrah
> I came with just enough gas
> But I had to do just one more pass
> Now I'm throttlin' back for the tanker track
> And tryin' to make it over the line

Dropped off the boom and I went forth
Asked if I could go a little further north
Said, "No problem man just tell me where the bad guys are"
They were FACing us in street by street
We were rollin' in, cleared hot on Tikrit
And ol' Bitchin' Betty she said I'd gone too far

> CHORUS

> Yeah, if I got an ounce of gas I'll take it
> If we climb high enough we just might make it

> CHORUS

12-29

Fuel You Ain't Got   *Chris "Snooze" Kurek*

Bingo Over Baghdad - This song is 100% truth put to music. In Operation Iraqi Freedom once we started pushing up north around Baghdad on our Killer Scout/SCAR/Armed Recce (or whatever the new term is these days) missions, gas became a precious commodity. In fact, for a 2-ship to locate and attack 8 separate targets and then RTB took every ounce of gas in the Viper. So much so that "bingo" fuel became merely a suggestion. For every hundred pounds below, we'd just say "Well, we'll just climb a little bit higher on RTB, no problem." I guess it worked 'cause no one flamed out trying to get home.

Clean rails

1215 A-10

CHORUS
A - 10, A - 10, A - 10, A - 10, A - 10
(Background singers repeat chorus throughout beneath lead singer's verses)

Gotta get my boots on, headin' out for Tucson
Thirty millimeter, she's a single-seater
Like a bayonet stabs, kickin' ass on a-rabs
This is gonna be fun, shootin' off my big gun
Mighty hard on tank treads, bustin' up some ragheads
Fillin' up my flight log, LUV my little Warthog

CHORUS

A-10 Thunderbolt II
The Hog

Warthog   *Col (Ret) Ken "Bat" Krause*
    Derided since its infancy by those unaware of its capabilities, the A-10 Thunderbolt II, affectionately known as the "Warthog" or, simply, "Hog" almost disappeared from the inventory in the jetwash of the Air Force sorting through its roles and missions as the Cold War wound down. "No European battleground," they said. "Too slow, and too vulnerable," whined others. When the military forces were whittled down to half of their mid-80s strength, the Hog was barely visible, mostly peeking out from under the covers of the reserves.
    But survive it did, and it has proven itself to be a tough, valued member of the Total Force. From Kosovo to Afghanistan to Iraq, the capabilities of the Warthog have won over critics from all services. No longer considered just a gun with a few airfoils strapped to it, the A-10 gained a deserved reputation as a devastating close air support friend. It can rain hellfire down on armored or entrenched unbelieving combatants, using MKs of all sizes, rockets, Mavericks, and CBU.
    But its most fearsome and deadly weapon is the Avenger GAU-8 30-mm gatling gun spewing out HEI or depleted Uranium anti-armor rounds. It makes dust piles out of concrete structures, scrap metal piles out of rolling armor, and road kill out of those who think carrying an RPG makes them invincible.
    The venerable and reliable A-10 and those who fly her will stand tall when warriors of all brands are counted. We've proved to all that having a calendar instead of an airspeed indicator doesn't mean you can't kick ass when called.

$\{$ ❦ ❧

. . . the mindset of a female combat pilot . . .
                                        Kat "BD" Burkhead
    There is no difference. I don't see myself as a female combat pilot — I'm merely a combat pilot. I think Harb, Coyote, Sassy, and Duke will tell you the same — it has nothing to do with the plumbing, though that is a bit of a bitch on 16 hour flights ;-) Gender is transcended in the air — as it should be.

1216 Nipple On the Grass

Air Force traditional. Arrangement and new lyrics ©2005 Dick Jonas. All rights reserved.

CHORUS (guys)
Hallelujah! Hallelujah!
Throw a nickel on the grass save a fighter pilot's ass
Hallelujah! Hallelujah!
Throw a nickel on the grass and you'll be safe

The airlines pay the big bucks, they've left the force a wreck
The Air Force needs more pilots who're politically correct
So they wrote some brand new rules; it's now a brand new game
They're letting girls fly combat jets, the world just ain't the same
CHORUS (guys)

Don't say that girls don't do this; don't tell me why I can't
It's all a bunch of bullshit, no need to rave and rant
I'll show you when the shooting starts, I'll only need one pass
To pump a load of tritonal, straight up Saddam's ass
CHORUS (guys & girls - save a fighter pilot lass)

When it is that time of month, don't try to fuck with me
I'll shove a pair of scissors, straight up the place you pee
Just take me to the flightline when I got PMS
Show me where those bastards are, I'm gonna kick some ass
CHORUS (girls & guys - save a fighter pilot lass)

I love this goddam Vyper much more than I love sex
He comes first in this girl's life, and then this girl cums next
I can fly this essobee right up its own tailpipe
And when I let them bullets go, that's one less ass to wipe

CHORUS (girls & guys)
Hallelujah! Hallelujah!
Throw a nipple on the grass save a fighter pilot lass
Hallelujah! Hallelujah!
Throw a nipple on the grass and you'll be safe

12-33

Please don't think I'm funny because I have a pole
Just hold it nice and steady while I find the hole
Ask the folks who've been there, the times I saved their ass
I am a KC boomer, I'm good at passing gas

CHORUS (girls)
Hallelujah! Hallelujah!
Throw a nipple on the grass save a fighter pilot lass
Hallelujah! Hallelujah!
Throw a nipple on the grass you might get laid

I got a load of engines to haul a load of bombs
If you don't think I'll kick your ass, then fuckin' bring it on
You know with all that cordite, I'm gonna get a hit
Bone, Buff, or Spirit, it just don't make a shit
CHORUS (girls)

The world's a safer place to be, now that times have changed
With All-American women flying All-American planes
So take your little ass to bed, sleep well, for goodness sake;
Your female combat flyers are goddam wide awake!
CHORUS (girls)

. . . Ta-dot-ta-dot-dot-dot — TITS!!!

Harb & BD

Circumequestrating. Yer
female combat flyers are
goddam wide awake!

Safer World   *Dick Jonas*

I pity those ignorant, backward countries who have disenfranchised fifty percent of their population. Think of all the wasted talent, all the progress not made, simply because the powers that be have decreed that women shall not stand shoulder to shoulder with men in pursuing life, liberty, and happiness. Damn shame.

I love America; and I admire her women beyond measure.

13

The Juvat Boys Choir
HEADHUNTERS

Audentes Fortuna Juvat

Fortune Favors the Bold

80th Fighter Squadron
United States Air Force

EROSONIC

Album Thirteen

THE JUVAT BOYS CHOIR
80th Fighter Squadron, U. S. Air Force
All these guys are alumni of the choir. They are all heard on the album. Left to right, they are Dale "Skin" Flick, Erik "Digger" Drake, David "Bull" Pittner, Jim "Tex" Ritter, Jay "JayBird" Riedel, Robbie "Shadow" Robbins, Don "Loco" Malatesta, Jim "Taz" Merchant, Tom "Nogas" Reichert, and Dick "Dixie" Corzine. Also on the album but missing from the picture are Jon "Meat" Tinsley and Dick "Elvis" Jonas.

1301 Twin-Tailed Lightning

In the jungles of New Guinea, the Headhunters carved their name
They were brave and they were fearless; downing Zeros was their
    game
From the beaches of Port Moresby, it was three miles to their 'drome
'Twas a dirt strip carved in a hillside; this is the place they called their
    home

    CHORUS
    Twin tailed Lightning was their warplane
    As they roamed Pacific skies
    Searching out the sons of Nippon
    Sending them to their demise

They were known not as a number; but as a name denoting fear
A tiny native was their logo, making history for all to hear
With names like Homer, Norb Ruff and Murphy, Cragg and Robbins,
    and Kirby, too
They swept the sky clean of the Jap menace
And came back victors when they flew
    CHORUS

They flew out from their airdrome, in their Lightnings climbing high
Looking up to find some Zeros; gonna blow them from the sky
All the odds were against them; all they had were their planes
And some friends down in the jungle, who made sure they'd fly
    again
    CHORUS

Making aces was their standard, two-hundred kills, even more

With fifty cal and twenty mic-mic, they always ran up their meatball

score

About the odds they never worried, from treetop level they'd cut 'em

down

And when they landed from their melees, they would drink and fuck

around!!

CHORUS (twice)

...JUVATS!!!

History *Robbie "Shadow" Robbins*

I wrote TTL for a going away, or "traditions," party at the Kun. JBC was OPR for the music; we wrote 3 to 5 new ones each month while I was there. I can't remember if it was me or another JBC member who chose the music for TTL. The lyrics were easy though. I'd grown up listening to Dad and Mom (Army nurse) talk to old friends about 3-Mile and Port Moresby. I was familiar with the history. Cragg, Robbins, and Homer were the first real wartime commanders. I added Ruff, Murphy, and Kirby because I had met them all and knew their names since I was a little kid.

P-38 Lightning

WWII Headhunter workhorse. More like a sleek racehorse, only deadlier. Dick Bong became America's all-time Ace of Aces in her.

1302 My Grandpa's a Fighter Pilot

My grandpa's a fighter pilot, what do you think about that
He flew Corsairs in World War II, he barely made it back
He shot down several Zeros, and after he was done
He went back to Kentucky, 'cuz he had a farm to run

> And some day if I can; I'm gonna be a fighter pilot just like
> that old man

My old man's a fighter pilot, what do you think about that
He flew F-4s in Viet Nam, he never made it back
For twelve long years he fought there, it's where he met his wife
He settled in the Philippines to lead a quiet life

> And some day if I can; I'm gonna be a fighter pilot just like
> that old man

Now I am a fighter pilot, what do you think about that
I flew the 'Vark in Turkey, I flew it in Iraq
Now I fly the Viper, with missiles, bombs, and gun
And some day when he's ready, I'll give it to my son

> And some day if he can; he's gonna be a fighter pilot just
> like his old man
> And some day if I can; I'm gonna be a fighter pilot just like
> my old man
> And some day if I can; I'm gonna be a fighter pilot just like
> that old man

13-5

Legacy   *Tom "Nogas" Reichert and Scot "Stain" Glass*

It was 4 Feb 04 and I was sitting in my hooch planning the next JBC practice. In walks Scot "Stain" Glass, guitar in hand. JBC auditions were to be held during our practice and Stain, an extraordinarily good guitar picker, was a shoo-in — if he could come up with the entry fee (write a song). But Stain was suffering from a serious case of writer's block, so we started tipping back a few cold ones and talking about possible song material. After the first six-pack was gone without one good idea we settled in for the duration (read that, raided the neighbor's fridge for more beer).

Stain started strumming a catchy tune on his guitar and I asked him what it was. He told me he'd heard it on a Saturday Night Live rerun; it was called *My Old Man's a Refrigerator Repairman*. He sang the song; it was pretty funny. I commented it was too bad his Dad wasn't a fighter pilot because the song would practically write itself. I just about fell out of my chair when he told me his grandfather was a WW II Corsair pilot, and his father was a pilot as well — flying for the "Company" during Viet Nam.

The song did write itself. Twenty minutes later Stain's mostly accurate autobiography was in the can. His first performance at Bruni's for his audition was memorable, and the song has gone on to become a fighter pilot staple. Pretty cool to be part of something that great.

F-4U Corsair

WWII Navy and Marine Corps ace!

1303   Yankee Air Pirate In Me

Seven Air Cobras on a fighter sweep; the flight lead soon fell out
Lt Brown took the remaining six, as the Punks drove that fight no
doubt
The 80th's first mission was soon complete; they landed their planes
in the hills
So get ready and raise that whiskey glass, as the Punks got all six
kills

> CHORUS
> They sang "Sammy Small", "Fireman's Song"
> "Twin-Tailed Lightning", "Kun Songs by the Sea"
> With their glasses raised, a "Fighter's Toast"
> To the "Yankee Air Pirate in me!"

In came Captain "Porky" Cragg, a leader who got in the fight
"I'll be dammed if those Friends or Tooeys take the Lightning before
my eyes"
The next morning he climbed into "Porky 1", to "talk" to the powers
that be
And two weeks later those Headhunters left, to fly their brand new
Lockheed

> CHORUS

Sixteen Hunters 1944, 38's climb in the night
That night attack on those Japanese ships, was the scariest most
would fly
Rolling in to make his very last pass, O.J. Harris took the first hit
And all was lost if not for the natives, who saved him from the Jap
menace

> CHORUS

13-7

A Million stories, some never told, only written in a song

But one day soon we'll hear them there in that Headhunter Heaven

above . . .

CHORUS x2 (Quiet then Loud)

The Punks   *Bruce "Big Fella" MacLennan*
        In late 1942 the 8th Fighter Group was about to be
equipped with the Lockheed P-38 Twin-Tailed Lightning. The
Group Staff had determined that only one of the squadrons would
be given the new aircraft. The 35th and 36th were old and respected units whose lineage traced back to before WW I. The 80th
would not be in the running for this honor.
        Capt "Porky" Cragg, the 80th's Commander, flew to the
8th FG headquarters in Port Moresby, New Guinea, to personally
consult with the powers that be about the decision. Less than two
weeks later, the 36th FS relieved the 80th; and in February 1943
the entire 80th Squadron moved to Mareeba, Australia, for con-
version to their brand new P-38s.
        It's my belief that this song was composed to commemo-
rate Capt Cragg's feat of stealing/looting/pirating the first P-38s
in the Group from the two other squadrons — the Friends and the
Tooeys — for the 80th. In song they allude to him, and themselves
by association, as a *Yankee Air Pirate!*

B-38 Lightning

Porky I's progeny. Heritage Flight, Davis Monthan AFB AZ, 5 Mar 05.

1304   Death Rains Down

In memory of Lt Gen Jay T. Robbins.

(Well it) started way back in '42, at a place called Mitchell Field
We were headin' off to fight a war didn't know what it would yield
We were green and we were new to the game but we were ready for a fight
We knew some of us weren't comin' back, we said that's all right
      We flew out of Moresby, strafin' Zeros on the way
      We flew at Hollandia, killing Nippons in the fray
      We are the Headhunters, with a history strong and proud
      We'll see you around, when death rains down

(There) was a man named "Porky" Cragg, led a squadron to
      its fame
We had friends who brought us back to the fight and they gave us
      our name
They were saviors in the jungle, their name denoting fear
The Nippons are gonna get their ass kicked cause the Headhunters
        are here
      We flew over Wewak, strafin' Zeros on the way
      We flew in the Lightning, killing Nippons in the fray
      We are the Headhunters, with a history strong and proud
      We'll see you around, when death rains down

(Well) "Porky""Cragg flew his last flight in a sad twist of fate
Jay T. Robbins was next in line, he was our saving grace
He taught the Headhunters how to fight, 22 kills of his own
And even now he looks down upon us, we are his second home

We flew out of Nadzab, strafin' Zeros on the way
We flew in the Lightning, killing Nippons in the fray
We are the Headhunters, with a history strong and proud
We'll see you around, when death rains down
His name was "Cock" Robbins, 22 Kills on the way
He flew in the Lightning, killing Nippons in the fray
He is a Headhunter, with a history strong and proud
We'll see him around, when death rains down
We'll see him around, in a lonesome cloud

Jay T. Robbins and "Jandina"

Tribute   *James "Taz" Merchant*

The Juvats were born out of the Headhunters and owe their legacy, doubly so, to Jay T. "Cock" Robbins. Quick background for the uneducated is that Cock was the successor to Porky Cragg " . . . in a sad twist of fate . . ."

Well; about 30 plus years later, Cock (then Lt Gen Robbins) was well connected and got wind that the 80th was being deactivated. The boys in the squadron, already prepping for the change to the 389th (not Juvats), got their patches sewed on their uniforms. However, when the news came down from on high that the 80th was *not* going to be deactivated, the boys put the old patch on the same spot after ripping off the 389th patch. While tearing the old patch off, the "Juvat" (of "Audentes, Fortuna, Juvat" — Latin for "Fortune Favors the Bold") was left on the sleeve. So now you have the picture of the 80th FS patch with no writing associated with it and a "Juvat" on the bottom. From then on the Juvats were . . . THE JUVATS!

So there's the background. Now the song.

Then Capt Michael "Spades" Waite was the JBC lead when we got the words on Gen Robbins passing. Without really any of our awareness in the JBC, he started writing up a song as a tribute to the man who had been so influential in the 80th's history. As he was nearing a final draft he asked then Lt Andy "Stinger" Scott, then Lt Dave "Fuge" Epperson and myself to help him polish off a bottle of Jack and finish up the song for the next JBC rehearsal.

The following week, we performed it — not for hire. And it was actually kind of eerie; because, with the exception of the tribute to Jeb Stuart, no one is ever somber (or even sober) at a JBC performance. Everyone just kind of took it in, and we had a moment of silence.

Spades then taught us about the "throw a nickel on the grass" tradition as he passed out nickels to the crowd and then talked about the bit of superstition that started the tradition where guys would "throw a nickel on the grass to save a fighter pilot's ass." We all went outside, tossed the nickel into the grass, and pretty much everyone said a little prayer to themselves for Gen Robbins. From then on it was almost a legendary song. Some said would rival the importance of TTL ("Twin-Tailed Lightning") in Juvat/Headhunter history.

Jay T. Robbins and "Jandina IV"

Note the 22 kills.

1305 Hit the Jets a-Runnin'

In June of 1950 the Commies headed south
They had a lot of bullets they had a lot of mouth
They gave the Deuce some business they had a big game plan
We met 'em at the 38th and there we kicked their can

> CHORUS
> We hit the jets a-runnin' boys and headed for the skies
> We fought 'em at the Yalu, and there the bastards died
> Ba da da dum - bum - bum, Ba da da dum - bum - bum

Number one he checked them in and said let's make 'em green
I got a tally-ho at ten, we'll hit 'em here unseen
He pushed the throttle to the wall, his jet let out a scream
Another commie bastard, went down in his machine
> CHORUS

The boys, a four ship on patrol, the lead was clean and young
He turned the flight to face the threat, the odds were 12 to 1
We burned, we turned, we whooped their ass! We made 'em taste
    our guns
And if you don't believe it, ask Kim Il Fucking Sun
> CHORUS

The war it finally ended we had an ace or two
Now we shoot the AMRAAM, we're droppin' GBUs
We've got a little Viper, they're shaking in their shoes
And all the goddam commies, still sing the fuckin' blues
> CHORUS

13-11

Now we're here in 2005, the commies still exist

They stand behind the DMZ and shake their faggot fists

They're chickenshit, they're scared as hell! They'll always make a
   fuss

And if the assholes press on south they'll have to fuck with us
   CHORUS x 2

... and there the bastards died ... *Don "Loco" Malatesta*

This song combines a little history, a little fiction, and a lot of gung-ho, bad-ass, fighter pilot attitude. It chronicles the Korean War and those heroic Headhunter aviators who stopped the Communist advance. They pushed the enemy back to the Yalu River, across which the MiGs fled to sanctuary when things didn't go their way — which was often.

Korea remains a powder keg — SAMs, AAA, and thousands of 'grunts' (infantry, God bless 'em!) ready to slam live magazines into their weapons and 'whup some Commie ass.' The 'Deuce' in the first verse refers to the U. S. 2nd Infantry Division, which remains in Korea to this day.

North of the DMZ is a bunch of North Koreans who have about the same unfriendly intentions towards us as we do toward them. It is still a war zone; no armistice has never been signed. Kim-Jong-Il, son of Kim-Il-Sung, continues to shake his fist at us and "make a fuss" with formidable, possibly nuclear weapons.

But, you know what? The Headhunters — Juvats — are still down there at the Kun, singing this song, their jets and their attitudes pumped up, ready to "make 'em green" if the Commies are stupid enough to press on south again.

F-86 Sabre
What killed the bastards.

1306   Strafin' 'Round the Mountain

Author unknown. Air Force traditional. Via Bill Getz in *The Wild Blue Yonder*. Arr ©1997 Dick Jonas. All rights reserved.

Now listen all you airmen, young and old
To the tales of fighter pilots, young and bold
With their fighters painted yellow
Leaping off to contact Mellow
In the crisp Korean air so blue and cold
> It was dive bomb old Sinanju, stop the Reds
> Eight 1000-pounders loaded, instant heads
> Four birds lined up on the runway
> Wish I'd gone to church on Sunday
> Hope we catch those lousy Commies in their beds
Twenty-thousand over Pyongyang, on northwest
Gas Mask Flight about to face the acid test
'Til at last the Yalu River
Which makes my liver quiver
With flak guns lined up twenty-four abreast
> Dust clouds roll up from Antung cross the way
> Twenty swept-wing Chinese warbirds out to play
> Thirty-sevens, twenty-threes
> All lit up like Christmas trees
> Salvo off the tip tanks; leap into the fray
Kimpo Tower clears the pattern with great haste
Twenty victory rolls our pilots do with grace
It was thrilling, it was hairy
Near that privileged sanctuary
Syngman Rhee will soon be boss of this whole place

Kimpo Tower, this is Gas Mask Willie Four

I am heading home, I'm through with this damn war

I am flying on to K-2

Heading one-five-oh for Taegu

'Cause they're sending back to Moscow for some more

Paradox *Dick Jonas*

Three of the top luminaries of Korea's air battles survived the war victoriously, only to lose their lives in the peace which followed. The leading ace of the war was Joe McConnell with 16 kills. He died testing a new version of the F-86 Sabre.

Iven C. Kincheloe finished the war with 10 kills. Assigned test pilot duty afterwards, he died in the crash of his F-104 chase plane. The plane lost power right after takeoff, too low for him to eject safely. He got out of the airplane, but plunged into the burning wreckage.

Jim Jabara was America's first jet ace in Korea. He finished the war with 15 victories. He was killed in an auto accident while enroute to a new assignment.

Fate somtimes conflicts with expectation. The WU calls that a paradox.

© 2001 KeithFerrisArt.com

F-86 Sabre

Leap into the fray!

1307   Korean Waterfall

Beside a Korean waterfall one bright and sunny day
Beside a shattered Sabre jet a young pursuiter lay
His parachute hung from a nearby tree, he was not yet quite dead
So listen to the very last words the young pursuiter said

"I'm going to a better land where everything is bright
Where whiskey flows from telephone poles, play poker every night
We haven't got a thing to do but sit around and sing
And all our crews are women, Oh death!, where is they sting?"

Oh death were is thy sting
Oh death were is thy sting
The bells of hell will ring-a-ling-a-ling . . .
For you, but not for me

Oh ring-a-ling-a-ling-ling, blow it out your ass
Ring-a-ling-a-ling-ling, blow it out your ass
Ring-a-ling-a-ling-ling, blow it out your ass
Better days are coming bye and bye!

. . . BULLSHIT!!!

. . . the bells of hell . . . *Bruce "Big Fella" MacLennan*

This song probably commemorates the loss of a member of a very close group of old fighter pilots who thought that they were invincible, and their young replacements, as they flew their F-86 Sabres out of bases in Japan in the first days of combat over Korea. They went out day after day to encounter the invading North Koreans, usually coming home victorious and unscathed.

Flying day only aircraft, they were normally at the O' Club by 1700 after having flown 2 or 3 missions. They had all the benefits of flying their missions out to hundreds of miles away, and then returning to hot food, hot showers, clean sheets, abundant whiskey and ever-running poker games. They had it made!

And then, all of a sudden, one of them didn't come back. And no one knew why. Had he been shot down? Had he spun out? Had he gone straight in?

Every one of those guys were affected by the loss. So, in typical fighter pilot fashion, a song had to be created. Each member added his feelings in a verse, or portion thereof, as if these would be *their own* last words.

The thing that's most poignant about the song is the venue everyone subscribed to. "Beside a Korean Waterfall, one bright and sunny day . . ." is apparently where each of them wanted to meet the sting of death. And they were right — better days *were* coming, bye and bye . . .

F-86 Sabre

O Death, where is thy sting!?

1308   Air Force 801

Author: Bill "Romeo" McCrystal. *via Bill Getz in "The Wild Blue Yonder,"and the Air Force Museum, Dayton, Ohio.*
Arr ©2005 Dick Jonas. All rights reserved.

Listen to the rumble, hear old Merlin roar
I'm flying over Moji like I never flew before
Hear the mighty rush of the slipstream, hear old Merlin moan
I'll wait a bit and say a prayer and hope it gets me home

Itazuke Tower, this is Air Force 801
I'm turning on the downwind leg, my prop is overrun
My coolant's overheated, the gauge says one-two-one
You better get the crash crew out and get 'em on the run

Air Force 801, this is Itazuke Tower
I cannot call the crash crew out, this is their coffee hour
You're not cleared in the pattern, now that is plain to see
So take it on around again, you ain't no VIP

Itazuke Tower, this is Air Force 801
I'm turning on the base leg, I see your biscuit gun
My engine's running rougher, the coolant's gonna blow
I'm gonna buy a Mustang, so look out down below

Now listen, Air Force 801, this is Itazuke Tower
We'd like to let you in right now but we ain't got the power
We'll send a note through channels and wait for a reply
'Til we get permission back, just chase around the sky

⋮ ♪ ❀ ❀ ❦ ❀ ⋮

13-17

Itazuke Tower, this is Air Force 801
I'm turning base-to-final, I'm running on one lung
I'm gonna land this Mustang, no matter what you say
I'm gonna get my chart squared up before the Judgment Day

Now listen, Air Force 801, this is Itazuke Tower
We're trying hard to help you, just give us one more hour
Patience is a virtue, as fighter pilots know
So be a good guy, listen up, we'll tell you where to go

Itazuke Tower, this is Air Force 801
I'm calling from the Great Beyond, my flying days are done
I'm sorry I exploded, I didn't make the grade
I guess I should have waited 'til the landing was okayed

Hello, Air Force 801, this here is Judgment Day
You're up in pilot's Heaven, and you are here to stay
You just bought a Mustang, you really bought it well
And Itazuke Tower, we sent 'em straight to Hell!

Air Force 801   *Dick Jonas*
        The following is posted in the Air Force Museum on a
large plaque with the words to Bill McCrystal's famous song. In
the JBC rendition, the very last line was modified by Mary
Jonas, a fighter pilot's wife with very keen perception.
        "During the general period of the Korean conflict in the
early 1950s, most personnel assigned to the Far East Air Forces
heard (and many sung) a humorous song which became known
by the misnomer <u>Itazuke Tower.</u> In reality, when the lyrics were
composed by Lt. William F. McCrystal in late 1948, his original
title was <u>Air Force 801</u>. This referred to P-51D serial number 44-
73<u>801</u>, the airplane assigned to Lt. McCrystal when he was
stationed at Itazuke Air Base, Japan, with the 80th Fighter
Squadron Headhunters."

1309   Yankee Air Pirate

I am a Yankee Air Pirate
With DTs and blood-shot eyeballs
My nerves are all run down from bombing Downtown
From SAM breaks and bad bandit calls

CHORUS

A Yankee Air Pirate, a Yankee Air Pirate
A Yankee Air Pirate am I
A Yankee Air Pirate, a Yankee Air Pirate
If I don't get my hundred, I'll die

I've carried iron bombs on the outboards
Flown high CAP for F-One-Oh-Thuds
I've sniveled a counter or two once or twice
And sweated my own rich red blood

CHORUS

I've been downtown to both bridges
To Thai Nguyen, Kep, and Phuc Yen
And if you ask me, then I'm sure you can see
There's no place up there I ain't been

CHORUS

Politically correct?

In today's mad scramble for ethnic distinction, I sincerely hope my own special minority does not get left out. I was born and bred deep in the heart of Dixie, somewhere south of George Wallace, and north of Jimmy Buffet. I am a proud, pedigreed redneck. And I'm sensitive about it.

(ref Eccl 93050601)

... And some of us ain't Yankees, a'tall ...

1310   Son Of Woody Juvat

CHORUS
(Well) I'm a Juvat, from the Wolfpack, and I fly the F-16
All the way from the whiskey arch, and north to the DMZ
I'm one of Porky Cragg's young pups and I'm mean as I can be
I'm a son of Woody Juvat and I fly the F-16

From war to war our presence is felt, no matter where we fly
We're mean as hell, we'll kick your ass, just give us a reason why
We'll drive your dicks into the dirt, and make you know we're here
Until you've faced a Juvat, you don't really know 'bout fear

Listen up you Commie fucks, in West PAC and the world
We're on call, day or night, we'll deliver to your door
We are the Juvat Wrecking Crew, destruction is our game
We'll also blow away your MiGs, the fee works out the same
                    CHORUS (. . . one of ol' Cock Robbins' boys . . .)

Kimichi-eatin' Kim Jong Il, you mother fucker you
Send your MiGs into the South, we'll mail them back to you
We don't have time for amateurs, and we're a hostile bunch
So if you want to start a war, you'd better bring your lunch

We like to drink and screw around, and run the whores downtown
Gamble and watch fuck flicks, until the crack of dawn
But if you think that makes us weak, just start your trip to Seoul
We'll strap our Vipers to our backs, and Fox 3 your asshole
                    CHORUS (. . . one of good ol' JayBird's boys . . .)

. . . a hostile bunch . . .   *Jon "Meat" Tinsley*

The song "Son of Woody Juvat" was a JBC take off the fighter pilot classic *Son of Satan's Angels*. As is tradition, if there are older lyrics that reference another fighter, the JBC will rewrite them to reflect their pride in the F-16. I'm not exactly sure who penned this particular version, but it speaks to the heart of every Juvat Viper Driver. This song has a particular in-your-face tone, with a whole lot of attitude, and also has specific geographical and personal references that make it relevant to the Korean peninsula.

The reference changed from Kim Il Sung after his death, to Kim Chong Il. The bottomline is that, the 80FS is a professional group of fighter pilots who train hard and know they are ready for anything that the North Koreans could throw at them. An interesting tidbit is that in the last line of the fourth verse the weapon referenced has changed as the mission of the 80FS has changed. The lyrics have evolved from Rockeye (CBU-20) to Magnum (AGM-88) and now Fox-3 (AIM-120 AMRAAM).

!! Meat !!

Token "hostile" from the bunch.

1311 Drag Index On the Rise

I see a bad configuration, this jet looks like a bowling ball
When will we cease this aggravation? Dream on, the tanks will
    never fall

CHORUS (Wing tanks)

I don't wanna fly, with wing tanks by my side
The drag index is on the rise

I hope I have a burner blowout, just as my gear begins to rise
Then I can dump them in the ocean, and see how those mother-
    fuckers fly

CHORUS (Wing tanks)

Now we have got an ECM pod, it's loaded up on station five
I hope I land right on the cable, and bust that fucker open wide

CHORUS (Pod on Station 5)

I don't wanna fly, with a pod on station five
The drag index is out of sight

Oh, boss, please don't think I'm bitchin'. I know it's not that you don't care
I feel my trigger finger itchin', my soul was meant for air to air

CHORUS (Wing tanks)
. . . CHORUS (Pod on Station 5)

8th Fighter Wing
. . . Kunsan AB ROK . . .

. . . don't think I'm bitchin'. . .   *Dick "Dixie" Corzine*

I arrived at the Kun in the spring of 1983 to find brand new F-16 Block 15's. Most of them had less than 300 hours — they even smelled new.

I was ecstatic! We flew air-to-air **CLEAN!!** We flew SAT/Range rides with a centerline and TERs on stations 3 & 7. At that time our recommended combat load was a centerline with MK-84s on 3 & 7 with AIM-9Ls on the wingtips. In this configuration the jet maneuvered like a dream. We were "Gods of the Air" over Korea.

In a few months wing tanks showed up on the Range birds. Maintenance quickly figured out that if they put wing tanks on every jet, any jet could fill any line in the schedule. Within weeks wing tanks were hardwired on every jet. After a few weeks of scheduling meeting fights, our range jets had wing tanks, the Air-to-Air jets had centerlines, and *all* spares had wing tanks. Our sleek little Falcon was starting to look a lot like a Phantom! I doubt maintenance appreciated the phonetic similarity.

A few months after that, the ALQ 131 ECM pods found their way to station 5. Now our light-weight fighter looked like a bowling ball — or, truly like an F-4 with crap hanging from every hard point on the aircraft. As a scheduler, I tried to explain to maintenance the difference between driving a Ferrari or a Gravel Truck. To no avail, because to them "a jet is a jet." However, we quickly learned that the ECM pod was so big that if you landed on the cable it would jump up and slap the pod, causing the ECM shop to pull the pod off the jet for inspection and testing that lasted about a week. Being standard innovative Headhunters, we figured out you did not really need to land on the cable and hurt the pod, all you had to do was tell maintenance you *thought* you landed on the cable, and they took the pod off, reducing your drag index about 25%.

We also figured if the Commies headed south, half the lines the first day would have burner blow-outs and dump the tanks. Using these two techniques we figured we could keep about 8 jets clean for Air-to-Air and the rest could keep tanks and pods to go North of the DMZ.

Next we got counseled for bitching about flying the jets in our "Wartime Configuration." Hence the verse about bitching. The point is, in the spring of '83 the Viper was a sleek, nimble, maneuverable little jet. By the summer of '84 our "Little Gray Jet" looked like a *bowling ball*!!

I tried, but could not find anyone who remembered who actually wrote this song. A couple of us remember helping to wordsmith it after a few beers one night in the hooch. I can't even remember if it was a choir meeting or just guys in the hooch. I do remember there was alcohol involved.

Tank Storage Facility

. . . My soul was meant for air-to-air . . .

1312   Freedom Bird

It's a shit hole, South Korea
Binjo ditches, blinding stench of Kimchi
Girls are cheap here, and riddled with disease
Five thousand won they'll drop right to their knees

> CHORUS
> Freedom bird, take me home, to the place I belong
> USA, round-eyed women, take me home, freedom bird

Drunken nights have, come and gone here
Puking Soju, passed out in the gutter
Cold and drafty, is the bathroom floor
How the hell I got here I couldn't find the door
> CHORUS

Flying Vipers, in Korea
Killing hornets, rolling in on Eagles
Low and fast now, scaring DAKs below
Push it up to Mach and watch that burner glow
> CHORUS

I hear the horn, in the morning hour it calls me
Big Lips announces that we are Condition Blue
And pulling on my mask I get the feeling that I should have gone on
leave today . . .
leave today-ay

CHORUS

. . . USA, back to the real world, it's time to go, Freedom Bird!

. . . the real world . . .   *Dale "Skin" Flick*

I don't know who wrote this song, but the guy was a fucking genius! It was one of the most requested tunes of the JBC on many a night at Brunigan's. I think the song appeals to anyone who has spent time at the Kun on many levels. It seems to embody every red-blooded American fighter pilot's disdain for a society that wasn't his own, as well as capturing the pride in spreading the sound of freedom from the mighty Viper accross the ROK while keeping the Chonger at bay. This was really one of my personal favorites to sing when I was over there.

C-17 Globemaster III

Company air all the way

1313   We've Been Everywhere

Original song *I've Been Everywhere* by Geoff Mack. Parody lyrics

Well, I'm sittin' in the bar, out at Kunsan-by-the sea
When a trash hauler saunters in and parks his ass right next to me
He checks my goatskin shoulder and he asks me, "What is that?"
I say, "That's my squadron patch; I'm a Headhunter — a Juvat!"
He says, "You're a Juvat?! I think I've heard of you;
Say, where in the hell have you all been, and what did you all do?!"

JBC CHORUS
We been everywhere, Man; we been everywhere
We crossed the mountains bare, Man; we breathed the flak-filled air
Of Zekes we've had our share, Man; we been everywhere

Been to Mitchell Field, Brisbane, Lowood, Moresby
Dobodura, Nazdab, Morotai, Owi
Dulag, Tacloban, Mindinao, Leyte
Townsville, Oodnadatta, Kokoda, Wadbi
Borneo, Neomoot, Bogadjim, Madang
Wewak, Fiji, Marilinann, Kavieng
　　　　JBC CHORUS (. . . MiGs . . .)

We been to Taegu, Kwangju, Fuchu, Kunsan
Inchon, Osan, Pusan, Suwon
P-Y Do, Cheju do, Guam, Okinawa
Hachinohe, Morioka, Sendai, Wakkanai
Tachikawa, Itazuke, Niigata, Pohang
Kagoshima, Hiroshima, Ie Shima, hot dang!
　　　　JBC CHORUS (. . . SAMs . . .)

13-27

We been to Hanoi, Haiphong, Phuc Yen, Yen Bai
Lang Son, Hoa Lac, Phu Tho, Son Tay
Hoa Binh, Nam Dinh, Thai Binh, Bac Ninh
Thai Nguyen, Gia Lam, Viet Tri, Do Son
Thud Ridge, MiG Ridge, Northeast Railroad
In town, cross town, up town, down town
JBC CHORUS (. . . DAKs . . .)

We been to Seoul, Kimpo, Honolulu, Wake, Midway
Hong Kong, Bangkok, Baguio, Manila Bay
Hualien, Tainan, Taitung, Keelung
Chiayi, Hsin chu, Kaohsiung, Ping Tung
Saigon, Singapore, Tokyo, Taipei; Angeles city, all night, all day

JBC CHORUS (. . . death . . .)

. . . !! JUVATS !! . . .

Bell P-39 Q "Airacobra"   USAF Museum

P-39 Airacobra
One of the skeletons in our closet.

13-28

Where We Been   *Jim "Tex" Ritter*
    At a Headhunter Reunion in Phoenix, 2004, I had a bit
too much whisky. Digger Drake and I got this great idea: let's
get Jonas drunk and convince him to do a CD featuring the
history of the 80th. Well, we did. And he did. SUCKER!
"We've Been Everywhere" and the CD is designed to show
the world where we've been. The Headhunters have been
everywhere, at least in PACAF. From Mitchell Field in 1942 to
the present day Juvats in the Republic of Korea. Proud history. I
am so blessed to have shared in the legacy that is the 80th. Were
it not for my beautiful children, I'd be still at the Kun . . . (OK
that and 30 years and 20 pounds, and an intolerance for anything
over 7.2 [symmetrical] g's!).
    When I was 12, lying on a dirt bank on a sunny fall day,
I saw an F-100 flying over and conning so beautifully. I decided
that flying fighters was for me. On to college. It turned out to be
a left-wing, anti-American shithole. I decided that I *was* a fighter
pilot, and joined ROTC. My AFOQT scores qualified me for pilot
training. I had 20/20 eyes, but a .025 diopter for astigmatism
(limit was .020) sent me to nav training. Shit!
    Assigned to KC-135's at K. I. Sawyer, I found that the
base ophthalmologist liked scotch whisky. Eventually, I got an
eyesight waiver (go figure) and went on to pilot training.
Graduated in '73 and after 10 years (in "77- thank you, Tommy
Boy!) , I finally got an F-4. To Kunsan. Sierra Hotel! Got about
1000 hours in the Phantom, D's and E's. Taught at Fighter Lead-
In. Retired on April Fool's Day, 1988.
    Good times, and the fighter pilot tendency to downplay
bad times. Camaraderie. That, Punks, is the tie that binds us all
together. If you ain't been there, then you don't know — from
Long Island, to Virgin's Lane, to Dobodura, to K-13, to Korat, to
Tahkli, to the Hanoi Hilton, to Kunsan.
    Audentes Fortuna Juvat. She does. God bless us all!

Leadership   *Dick "Elvis" Jonas*
    Leadership has been defined as getting other people to do
your work for you. This album represented a great undertaking, a
task much larger than any one of us. True, I'm the producer, but I
could not have produced anything at all without the leadership
skills of Jay Riedel and Jim Ritter.
    Once we took the decision to get it done, we needed songs,
lyrics, singers and musicians. I had not seen Korea nor
participated in a JBC song fest for 20 years. I was *not* the man for
those jobs. JayBird and Tex were — and the rest is history.

JayBird

Tex

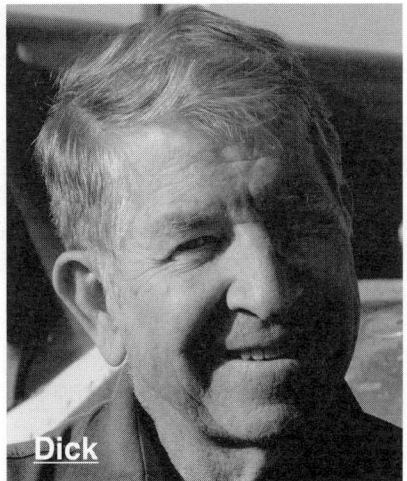

Dick

13-28.2

1314   Juvat History Song

I am just a Juvat but my story's often told
In the bars through the pacific
The tales are of woe and friends that sometimes die

The commies laugh, but those fuckers hear what they want to hear
And disregard the rest . . . Do do doooooooo . . . Do do do do

From the jungles of New Guinea where Dick Bong had 40 kills
In the company of Juvats, with the roar of the lightning in the deep
       blue sky

Flyin' low, seekin' out the sons of ni-pon
They sent them to their graves, in another war an era passes by

Kim Il Sung came south to meet us in nineteen-fifty-one
And he got our answer, a hail of lead and death rained from our jets
       we're told

We lost good men, but the price they had to pay was rich in
deep red commie blood . . . Do do doooooooo . . . Do do do do

Juvats planned their deadly routes, along Thud Ridge in Nam,
       Vietnam
Bringin' death deep in the valleys where the bandits roamed
Bandits roamed, bandits roamed . . . do do do do

In the arches slept a Phantom Two, a fighter by her trade
And she carried out her heritage for 20 years, but she grew tired and
       very old
She cried out in her pride "I am leaving! I am leaving!
But my memory will remain" . . . do do do, do do do do

So Juvats hold your heads up high, your history does you proud
And the free world will remember
The brave and gallant men who paid the highest price

The Wolf Pack lives, and the Juvats keep on marching
With their vipers flying high, with a falcon's speed this era's just
    begun

Lai-la-lai, lai-la-lai-lai-lai-lai-lai, lai-la-lai . . . (. . . etc . . .)

Tradition and Commitment   *Bruce "Big Fella" MacLennan*
    This song was probably composed by the JBC in the early
'80s just as the squadron was transitioning to the F-16. The ven-
erable F-4 still populated the ramp and shelter arches, but Vipers were replacing them on a weekly basis.
    The remaining Phantom driver Choir members likely put
this one together as a tribute to its long and proud heritage in
the 8th Wing at Kunsan AB. Unique in this song is the respect
that today's Headhunters have for the bravery and competitive-
ness of their predecessors of forty years earlier. Their commitment to those standards is quite obvious in the lyrics.

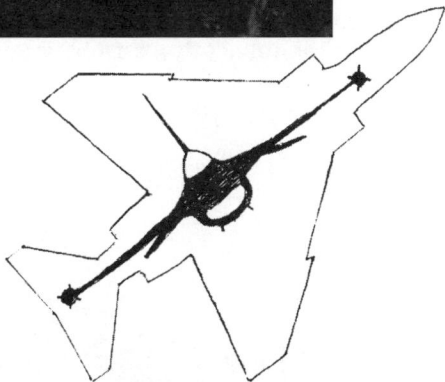

Twin-Tailed Lightning, Woody, Phantom/Viper
. . . your history does you proud . . .

13-30

Dick Jonas

Dick Jonas was born and raised in the Suwannee River valley of northern Florida.

He served four years as an infantryman in the Georgia Army National Guard while attending Valdosta State College. Upon graduation in 1965 he entered the Air Force, receiving his commission through Officer Training School. In 22 years service he flew 3,000 jet fighter hours in the F-4 and F-16. During 125 missions in Vietnam he earned the Distinguished Flying Cross with two oak leaf clusters and the Air Medal with 12 clusters.

After retirement from the Air Force, in 1986, he became an Aerospace Science Instructor in the Air Force Junior ROTC program.

During 1991 and 92, in 325 performances he played the leading role in *Guv: The Musical*, a stage production of the Mill Avenue Theater in Tempe, Arizona.

Dick retired from the teaching profession after 15 years of service, in June 2004. He is now a fulltime entertainer and music producer. His aim is to preserve and perpetuate the legacy of America's warrior musicians —

The songs we sang about the planes we flew and the people we knew in the wars we fought.

He is known as "America's Foremost Military Aviation Song Writer and Balladeer." He has produced fourteen albums of his kind of music, and published a book entitled *RBAAB: The Red-Blooded, All-American Boy,* containing song lyrics and war stories for the first six CDs.

This book, *PTF: Passing the Flame,* covers the songs and background on albums #7 through #13.

Dick is an actor, a writer, a guitar-player, a singer, and a businessman. He also flies.

He and his wife, Mary, reside in Chino Valley, just north of Prescott, Arizona.

<u>Epilogue</u>

This book and the CD albums which go with it came about because I woke up one day with the realization that I was *not* going to live forever. It struck like a thunderclap that, just as that day came when I flew my forever last operational sortie in a high performance jet fighter, another day was bearing down when I would write my last poem, strike my last chord, and sing my last song.

It is time to pass the flame.

The CDs and song books are available by mail order from EROSONIC, Box 1226, Chino Valley, Arizona 86323. They are also available at amazon.com. There's more information at the EROSONIC website, www.erosonic.com.